# The Scars We Carry

## How to Overcome Relationship Abuse to Mend Your Heart and Soul

### Zilla Carina

First published by Ultimate World Publishing 2024
Copyright © 2024 Zilla Carina

ISBN

Paperback: 978-1-923255-36-4
Ebook: 978-1-923255-37-1

Zilla Carina has asserted her rights under the Copyright, Designs and Patents Act 1988 to be identified as the author of this work. The information in this book is based on the author's experiences and opinions. The publisher specifically disclaims responsibility for any adverse consequences which may result from use of the information contained herein. Permission to use information has been sought by the author. Any breaches will be rectified in further editions of the book.

All rights reserved. No part of this publication may be reproduced, stored in or introduced into a retrieval system, or transmitted in any form, or by any means (electronic, mechanical, photocopying, recording or otherwise) without the prior written permission of the author. Any person who does any unauthorised act in relation to this publication may be liable to criminal prosecution and civil claims for damages. Enquiries should be made through the publisher.

**Cover design:** Ultimate World Publishing
**Cover art**: Lisa Rowland 2023
**Layout and typesetting:** Ultimate World Publishing
**Editor:** Vanessa McKay

Zilla Carina
www.zillacarina.com

Ultimate World Publishing
Diamond Creek,
Victoria Australia 3089
www.writeabook.com.au

# Testimonials

"Wow! Life changing on so many levels of transformation and leading the way for so many women to feel empowered to take back control of their own lives. Zilla speaks from her heart with honesty and bravery to share her story. This is a must-read book!"

**Melanie Wood,
Publisher, Author and Speaker.**

"I genuinely believe 'vulnerability is the new leadership' and Zilla is leading that charge with this amazing piece of writing. The Scars We Carry is not a book… it's a scripture. One that, through story, will take you on a journey of self-reflection, self-enquiry, and most of all, self-ownership. Be ready and be brave because Zilla sure as heck was in writing this book and sharing this journey. Truly inspiring, truly transformational, and *deeply necessary reminder to us all to reflect, enquire and take ownership of the Scars We Carry."*

**James Balog,
Co Founder Ultimate Entrepreneur**

"Zilla's story will be relatable to many and gifts tremendous courage to the reader whose circumstance she validates. Offering practical tools and timeless wisdom, *The Scars We Carry* is for anyone who needs to recognize the situation they are in, and the importance of embarking on their personal journey to freedom."

**Kalyan Darsham,
Facilitator of transformation with yoga and meditation, astrologer**

"Zilla has given me the skills and guidance to live my best life. Her book is honest, heartfelt, and hard to put down. She is an inspiration and generous to share her story along with the many lessons on how we too can heal ourselves and live a better life."

**Jenn O, (Client)**

*"The Scars We Carry' is genuinely committed to unearthing the most free, aware and self-committed version of yourself by the time you read the last sentence. It is a journey that is impossible not to connect with. Each section allows you to drift off, heal your scars and, more importantly, take absolute charge of your future now."*

**Craig Vance,**
**Videographer and Photographer**

*"From the first sentence to the last, I could not put this book down. I felt like my heart was in coherence with the realness of Zilla's experiences. I am inspired by her courage and know that anyone reading The Scars We Carry will discover for themselves the many gems within the pages."*

**Nikki Butler,**
**Wellbeing Consultant and Trainer**

*Zilla's writing is something we can all learn from. I love this book and can see the impact it will have on so many people's lives!*

**Phil Hedges,**
**Founder and Creator,**
**EMT App and Mind Mechanics**

"Getting to know Zilla has been an eye-opening experience, revealing her deep passion and commitment to making the world a better place through her unwavering values. It's clear to me that her essence is rooted in a profound sense of fairness and compassion. Observing her approach to kindness has been truly inspiring—not merely superficial niceties, but a genuine, heartfelt kindness that uplifts and guides others. 'The Scars We Carry' is a vivid reflection of Zilla's journey through significant challenges and her remarkable ability to create a nurturing life for herself and her children amidst adversity. When I learned Zilla was going to be published, my excitement was boundless. My enthusiasm was not just for her achievement but for everyone who would be touched by her wisdom, enriching their hearts, minds, and lives. This book isn't just a read; it's an opportunity to connect with Zilla's gentle strength and insights. I highly recommend 'The Scars We Carry' to anyone looking for a story that combines resilience with a tender perspective on overcoming life's hurdles."

**Tyler Erikson, Founder and CEO, The Erickson Training Company**

*For my beautiful children, you inspire me to show up and be my best self every day. I love you both forever and always!* 💖

*In loving memory of my parents and grandparents, thank you all so much for your wisdom and unconditional love.* 💖

*For my amazing siblings, I couldn't have dreamed of better people to grow up with. I love you both so much.* 💖

# Contents

| | |
|---|---|
| Testimonials | iii |
| Foreword | 1 |
| Disclaimer | 5 |
| Introduction | 11 |
| CHAPTER 1: Your Journey Awaits | 15 |
| CHAPTER 2: What's the Mission? | 23 |
| CHAPTER 3: It's Your Choice | 31 |
| CHAPTER 4: My Defining Moments | 39 |
| CHAPTER 5: Oh No, Not Again | 53 |
| CHAPTER 6: The Vortex | 71 |
| CHAPTER 7: The Freshest Scars | 85 |
| CHAPTER 8: The Cracks Appear | 103 |

| | |
|---|---|
| CHAPTER 9: Golden Repair | 125 |
| CHAPTER 10: I am Me; I Am Love | 135 |
| CHAPTER 11: Living Life Now | 143 |
| CHAPTER 12: Choose Now | 153 |
| So, What Next? | 165 |
| About the Author | 169 |
| Speaker Bio | 173 |
| Further Reading | 175 |

# Foreword
## Tom Cronin

Through the journey of life, we often find ourselves entangled in the complexity of relationships, where love and pain coexist, and scars tell stories of resilience and transformation. Zilla Carina's compelling book, "The Scars We Carry – How to Overcome Relationship Abuse to Mend Your Heart and Soul" is a raw, vulnerable and yet powerful exploration into the depths of healing from the wounds inflicted by relationship abuse.

I had the honour of meeting Zilla through my work as a meditation teacher and coach. She came to me looking to find support through meditation after the intense challenges she had been through. In our time working together, I not only taught her to meditate, guided her through deep immersions on retreats, but also mentored her in my Zen Academy Leadership program and watched her grow into a powerful force of change in the world as an author, coach, and leader.

As I was reading The Scars We Carry, it dawned on me that nothing in Zilla's life has been wasted. Yes, she faced immense challenges, yes, she went through things you wouldn't want any woman to have to go through. However, Zilla has risen out of that dark abyss and is now a shining beacon of light, guiding other women in their dark night to find a way out. Zilla is a walking example of how we can turn tragedy into triumph, lead into gold, and dark nights into bright daylight.

With delicate and powerful writing, The Scars We Carry not only takes us into the moving and painful story of Zilla's personal life, but it also offers us a road map, a strategy, to help other women who might find themselves a victim of similar types of experiences. This is something needed in the world right now. Statistics from www.ourwatch.org in Australia alone suggest that two out of five women experience some form of abuse in their relationships, and in the year

## Foreword

2021/22, 5606 women (an average of 15 women a day!) were hospitalised due to family and domestic violence. It really is time we bring more awareness to this, where empowered women like Zilla help give voice to something that has been muted for far too long. It's women like Zilla who are playing a big part in changing the current status quo and hopefully preventing more of this pain and suffering.

In an ancient body of wisdom called The Vedas, there is a view that turbulence, chaos, disorder, pain and suffering are cues from the Universe to adapt and change. The longer we ignore the signals, the more extreme the signals become and the more extreme the pain. Adaptation is key to reduce the suffering. Tuning into that guidance system that is trying to show us another way of living and taking action is the path to peace. Zilla has shown us a way to adapt and change through not only her personal story but also the guidance that reveals a way to heal and move forward.

"The Scars We Carry" is essential reading, not just for women who are in or who have been in abusive relationships, but also for all of us, to help us be more aware of the extent of the pain and suffering that many women carry individually and collectively.

Zilla Carina's guidance transcends the ordinary, offering insights that empower readers to confront and overcome the challenges of violent and controlling relationships. Through shared stories, collective strength, and the wisdom embedded in these pages, may you find solace, courage, and the path to reclaiming your heart and soul.

Tom Cronin
Meditation Teacher, Author, Speaker, Coach

# Disclaimer

This book is a personal reflection on experiencing deep trauma, pain and betrayal on many levels. It is written purely from the author's own point of view and how it felt at the time. It is not a book of blame or shame, as we are all fallible and are a product of our own life experiences and conditioning, and we only know what we know at any moment in time.

Any persons referred in this book may be carrying their own scars and it is acknowledged that we all can only act with the knowledge and conditioning we have experienced in our lifetime. Any views expressed by the author, are purely from her standpoint and are not to be taken as everyone else's experience.

The author emphasises the importance of making choices and not dwelling in the pain. You are encouraged to take time to process the emotions and then gathering yourself to consider options. Life is a series of choices, and the author advocates for living from the heart, with love, integrity, and without fear. It is encouraged to seek support from others who can help identify opportunities and guide us to our personal freedom and happiness. The author reflects on her own mistakes and the lessons and strengths learned from them. The emphasis is placed on the power of making conscious choices and not getting trapped in the vortex of negative thoughts and patterns of behaviour. Ultimately, the author asserts that life's outcomes are influenced by internal and personal choices rather than external circumstances. The examples in this book are meant to highlight the importance of never giving up and of knowing there is always a way through, even in the most challenging situations, with dignity. It all starts with self-love and respect.

The author believes that most people on the planet want to live in freedom and harmony, and it is time to stand up and voice it far and wide. To do this, we must learn to say "NO MORE" to those who disrespect us. Whether that is a government or an individual seeking power and control. Either way, healing is our

# Disclaimer

own responsibility and starts from within. Once we heal, it ripples out to our near ones, our communities, and ultimately it will spread across the world. Imagine that. What would that feel and be like?

The information in this book is intended to help readers understand how we can choose to make positive changes for ourselves and our communities. It is based on the author's research, experience, and opinions. It is not a substitute for professional or medical advice.

Every effort has been made to ensure the accuracy of the information presented in this book at the time of publication. However, the author does not guarantee the accuracy, completeness, or usefulness of any information provided. Readers are encouraged to verify any information provided with other sources.

The information presented in this book is meant to be used for informational purposes only. Readers are solely responsible for their actions and decisions. The author and publisher shall have neither liability nor responsibility to any person or entity regarding any loss or damage caused, or alleged to be caused, directly or indirectly by the information contained in this book.

This book contains references to external books, websites and other resources. The author does not endorse or assume responsibility for the content of any third-party resources mentioned within this book.

This book is written from a place of love, and it is your choice to read on and do whatever feels right for you 🫶. It is your choice. Whatever it takes!

*Perhaps love is the process of my leading you gently back to yourself.*

~ **Antoine de Saint-Exupéry**

# Introduction

*It doesn't matter what's been written in your story so far. It's how you fill up the rest of your pages that counts.*
- **Jennifer Wagner**

Are you tired of *revolving*, finding the same type of partner, and re-living the same shitty patterns over and over again? If you are ready to say "enough is enough," then this book is for you. I'm going to be up front here and say I am not a psychologist, psychiatrist, psychic, or any other kind of 'psych' person. I do have a science degree, and love to experiment and use my experience, knowledge, and lessons learned from my almost sixty years on this planet.

# The Scars We Carry

One of my favourite questions is, *when is NOW a good time for change?* Often we tell ourselves, *not now, but……. when 'this' or 'that'!* Well, I ask you when will 'now' ever be the right time? How many empty apologies will you accept? How many empty promises will you wait for? How much are you willing and choosing to put up with? When will you start filling up the rest of your pages with conscious purpose?

Join the journey, it may even inspire you to start your own. It's not for the fainthearted as it meanders through the depths of the quagmire of life's challenges, hitting the emotional high of highs of falling and being in love, and deep into the despair of lost love.

Love! That floaty, beautiful, and uplifting feeling, that feeling like you've hit the jackpot. Until somewhere down the track, you realise you've arrived in hell. You are lost and stuck in the dark side of emotional and/or physical violence, with no way out.

The good news is there is a way to rewrite your story before it is too late. It has taken me almost half a century to work through the whole cycle and come out the other side. I have done the work, learned the lessons and come up with a plan to get yourself healed, find the right support, and move forward bolder and

## Introduction

braver than you ever thought possible. Join me in my journey to freedom, self-awareness and becoming a kick ass human being. Obviously, this story is not only for women, but men who have been trodden on and taken advantage of because they too have been 'too nice'. And perhaps, for some of you who are already on a path to changing your past ways and learning to live with the truth of who you have been and on your way to who you are now becoming.

Be prepared. You may experience some discomfort along the way. Just remember, it's a journey into navigating your way through stuff a hell of a lot quicker than I did!

Come one, come all, it's an incredible adventure.

## CHAPTER 1

# Your Journey Awaits

*Life is a journey, not a destination.*
**Ralph Waldo Emerson**

Congratulations! I'm so glad you've chosen to join this journey. It may just become a big step forward into your new life. In order to move through this, all you need is to have an open mind and heart, leave judgment of yourself and others at the front door and hopefully there will be a few 'gold nuggets' to collect along the way. Now, strap yourself in, grab a cuppa, juice or even a beer, whatever tickles your fancy and enjoy the ride.

The following passages are from the book *Standing at the Edge: Finding Freedom Where Fear and Courage Meet by Joan Halifax* (2018), who graciously allowed me to use the following words, for which I am truly grateful.

*"There is a Japanese practice called kintsukuroi, meaning 'golden repair.' Kintsukuroi is the art of repairing broken pottery with powdered gold or platinum mixed with lacquer, so that the repair reflects the history of breakage. The 'repaired' object mirrors the fragility and imperfection of life—and also its beauty and strength. The object returns to wholeness, to integrity."*

Just like pottery, a heart can be broken into so many pieces that it is sometimes difficult to function in daily life. I love that we can use the art of golden repair as a model of how we can mend something so broken and create something beautiful and strong. The following chapters depict many challenges we navigate, resulting in a wad of scars, and how certain skills and strategies can be learned and practised to emerge as a better version of ourselves. But we must make the choices to evolve and not revolve. To understand my journey a little better, I will fill you in on how I became who I am.

My Swedish roots go back as far as is currently traceable. I often romanticise that I am of noble and strong Viking stock. How else could I have made it through this lifetime so far? Indeed, our lineage is even believed to be connected to a Swedish King. I must check into this one day. I often think how interesting it is that many people don't know where they come from or who they are, which makes sense when you think about how easy it has become to travel anywhere in the world, particularly in the last century. These days, I identify more as a citizen of planet Earth than anything else. After all, we all come from this tiny dot of a planet amongst the vastness of the space around us. And on a side note, we need to pay more attention to what we can do to nurture our own home and communities.

My parents were nomads. Working in the airline industry had many benefits, including working and living in different countries. They were always looking for adventures and finding new horizons. In the early 1970s, we were about to move to Denmark for Dad's work when Mum received a call from the Australian Consulate in Stockholm. They had applied and been accepted for a program called Assisted Passage; a scheme promoted by the Australian Government. Mum couldn't wait for Dad to wake up from his night shift sleep! They had totally forgotten about it and had only had two weeks left to confirm whether they would accept the offer to move. After some brief conversations, they decided to do it, and shortly after, we were packed up and on our way to Melbourne, Australia. My parents deemed that the 'mandatory' two years stay would be worth the adventure.

And what an adventure it was! My brother and I learnt to speak basic English on the plane trip over. We arrived at the Immigrant Hostel in Melbourne and began our new life. We went to the hostel's English school and started primary school nearby. We were squished in a small two-bedroom unit. There was no kitchen, so every day we dined in the massive cafeteria for breakfast, lunch, and dinner. As you walked into the cafeteria, there was a type of 'foyer' which absolutely stunk of humid warm vomit. I do not know where it came from and the smell inside the cafeteria only slightly improved. Thankfully, it was not the same stench. All I remember is that it was so gross. The food was bland, cafeteria packed with people, and I quickly learnt to hold my breath every time I had to go through the entry.

Another memory that stands out from this time was when I was confronted by a man who wanted me to put my hand in his pocket as he had a gift for me! Whoa, I bolted home as fast as my little legs carried me. It was so surreal and icky, I had to ask myself several times, *did that actually, really, just happen?* It was disgusting. I was only six years old. I became quite wary of adults I didn't know and more aware of my personal space. A big lesson learned at a very early age.

Thankfully, it wasn't long before Dad and his work mate found work with a helicopter company in Sale near Ninety Mile Beach in rural Victoria. Our two families bought a caravan each and off we went. For six months, we called our caravan home parked by a river in a Caravan Park, where we even caught and smoked eels. Yum! Coming from city life in Sweden, the wildlife was exciting, albeit a little scary at the beginning with kangaroos, a myriad of singing bird life, tiger snakes, giant lizards and goodness knows what else.

We then moved back to, and lived in Melbourne for eight years, with a two-year break in the middle when we moved back to Sweden.

Five primary schools and one high school later, we had firmly planted our roots on Australia's beautiful Gold Coast, and never looked back. Mum and Dad had finally found their home, also known as their 'paradise'. Dad scored a job at Brisbane Airport that he held for the rest of his working life. I attended two more high schools, that's another story in itself, before commencing university and absolutely loved the relaxed lifestyle and people.

I grew up with my father encouraging me in everything I did and his mantra to me was, "you can do and achieve anything you set your mind to." Which I did. The mantra sure sank in and I believed it to my core. I achieved my Bachelor of Science Degree and embarked on my professional career with gusto. I started working as an Environmental Consultant and Scientific Officer and then branched into the occupational health and safety field and scored a great position with the State Government. It was a very male dominated world at the time and the construction industry was challenging. I stood up for myself on construction sites, in the office, and on the street. I warded off continuous sexual harassment on many levels. I was strong and stood my ground, but also had to finely balance it! I had this amazing feeling of power and strength inside me and at the time I fully believed I couldn't show it for fear of repercussions and ultimately being demoted or even losing my job. They weren't very progressive at all in those days. This feeling that I couldn't show my true self also emerged in my relationships. I feared losing my partner by somehow making them feel less of a man with this strength I bottled up inside. I know so many strong wonderful men now that truly love and respect the true strength of women. This is how I failed so miserably in my personal relationships. Why did I feel I had to put a lid on my inner power? My inner Captain Marvel was zapped to conform to the societal expectations of the time. Despite this, I did my best at work to become respected and soon started climbing the proverbial corporate ladder as far as I could, and I absolutely loved it!

I felt like I could make a positive impact, not only at the workplace but on a much greater scale. My grandiose dreams had begun to percolate and brew, but I had no idea how or when it would happen.

Q: What are your most significant events that have shaped your life so far?

Date: _____

_____

_____

_____

_____

_____

# CHAPTER 2

# What's the Mission?

*Walk slowly, but never backwards.*
**James Clear, Atomic Habits (2018)**

To answer the question, *What's the Mission?*, we need to go back again and identify where I started collecting the scars that have shaped my relationship life. First, I have to say that somehow I always had a boyfriend, ever since I was in primary school. Wow, I'd never really thought too hard about that one.

Having an older brother, there was no shortage of boys around my sphere. I remember, with a smirk on my face, how my brother wasn't too happy, as at times his friends seemed more interested in me than him. But that's another story.

I collected boyfriend after boyfriend, they weren't just short term either. It seemed whenever I found myself on my own, someone else I liked turned up on the scene. I experienced my first 'love' at fourteen, totally innocent (i.e., no sex), but the connection we had was incredible. He wrote poems and letters and songs for me, and I felt his love so deeply. We were so young. It only lasted six months, but felt so much longer at that age. The essence and feeling of that love has lasted my lifetime and it created an expectation that this was what love was meant to be like. I only ever once came close to that same feeling many years later, but my situation at the time and my head steered me away from taking that route. Take note, fatal mistake number one! Actually, that was number two, or was it three?

After my first long-term relationship—aged fifteen to eighteen—ended when I found out that I had been cheated on for the first time, I collected my first big scar. I quickly moved into another relationship that

## What's the Mission?

lasted four years. When that gut feeling returned, I found I was being cheated on again. I left and decided to be on my own and just finish my bachelor's degree in peace.

Of course, this didn't last long, and before I knew it, another suitor came into play. I had admired him from a distance. He was in a band and seemed so self-confident. He was handsome, had a brilliant voice, and I fell hard. We had a few ups and downs, mainly because I felt he still wasn't over his previous love, but we stayed together. We had been together for three years. I was in my late twenties, and I wasn't sure about the longevity of our union. So, I decided to have a talk about where our relationship was heading and perhaps we would go our separate ways. Instead, he turned around and proposed to me. I think I still have grazes on my chin from when my jaw dropped to the floor, thinking *what just happened? What the hell do I do now?* It went so differently to how I'd expected. I wasn't prepared, and so I didn't take the time to think about it.

Instead, I stood there gobsmacked, and said yes! I figured we were best friends, we loved each other, and we could make it work. Add this one to the scar tally! This was my first major questionable life decision.

We were living in Sweden at the time as I had always wanted to go back and live as an adult and make my own choice where in the world to live. We went adventuring through Europe whilst we were in that neck of the world and had the best times, and also a few not so great ones. We married in the historic town hall of my birthplace, with only a couple of close friends in attendance. My dream had always been to get married with family and friends present. His dream was different. He wanted to marry and have a big celebration when we eventually moved back to Australia. When we did eventually move back, the big celebration didn't happen. I had been offered a great job and went back into corporate work, whilst he stayed behind in Sweden to see out our apartment lease. We made our home in Brisbane and were enjoying a nice 'DINKs' (double income no kids) lifestyle and remained close and cared for each other deeply for many years.

The cracks showed up especially for me, when we lost a very close friend to a drug overdose. I really needed him to step up and be there for me, but for whatever reason, he couldn't, and things really turned for me at that point. Death affects us more deeply and on so many more levels than we realise. It was at this point that I knew deep down, things weren't feeling right.

## What's the Mission?

Almost a year later, and following a seven-day hike in the wilderness with my best girlfriend and some amazing souls we met on the way, I knew I couldn't stay in the relationship. Being in nature with no running water, cooking facilities, beds or comfort of any sort, really opens you up to yourself and shows you things that you would otherwise never see. It truly was and always will be one of the best and life changing experiences of my life.

Leaving him was the first hard decision of my life. It took six months to get the courage up to accept that I had to go, but I knew I had to. I couldn't take away the opportunity for him to find love again and long-term happiness. And likewise, I yearned for more. In my mind and heart, I feel that living in anything less than bliss, fun, and harmony is not why we are here. Aside from the odd disagreements, which are part of a healthy relationship, I believe that when you find your person, it should be 95 percent 'cruising' and adventures. This takes work, continuous unconditional love, nurturing, growth and especially open and honest communication.

Dad used to always say a marriage requires two things: communication and compromise, full stop. This type of compromise is not to be confused with sacrifice.

There is a significant difference. We all deserve to live ours dreams and we cannot be expected or be forced to live out or in someone else's dream. It is so important from the outset, once you get beyond the honeymoon phase, to be real and totally honest about what your dreams, goals and intentions are. Preferably before you go anywhere near that proverbial aisle towards marriage.

It is not an easy conversation to have, particularly when you have heart-shaped eyes and don't want to scare the potential 'love of your life' off! However, it must be done so you can both be open, honest and speak freely about the future. If one of you are not honest and open about your thoughts or don't take the conversation seriously, you will be predisposed to living a resentful and unhappy life together. Unfortunately, this became the norm for so many pre-baby boomers, and many boomers too. The idea that you should stay in a marriage because it was spoken in vows, likely written by someone else, or perceived as the right thing to do, is now archaic thinking.

Thankfully, the Gen-Xers started questioning this, and the paradigm started shifting. We saw more and more people making the choice to uncouple. Unfortunately, the skills it takes to do this successfully weren't as

## What's the Mission?

available as they are today, and many children suffered. Today's new age kids seem to be so much wiser to the destructive and 'old school' way of falling in line at all costs. I love this refreshing start to a new era of inclusion of all humans, no matter who they are or choose to be. It's so freeing that judgement, bullying and intimidation are slowly starting to be less of the norm and becoming more and more unacceptable. I am fully aware they do still exist; it just doesn't seem to be as brazen and toxic as it was. I am seeing more and more of an awakening into a brand-new world, and we are moving forward thanks to new and evolving knowledge and technology. This is a great thing, as we need to find solutions to current and future issues if we are to survive as a species on the planet.

So, there it is. An insight into where I'm coming from and guiding you to. Peace within equals peace without. My passion and mission are to encourage and guide self-healing, and to grow and nurture our ability to move forward with the right people in our lives to facilitate positive personal, community, and global connections.

Q: What are the three top non-negotiable things you do for yourself (no one else)?

Date: _____

_____

_____

_____

_____

_____

# CHAPTER 3

# It's Your Choice

*Love is always the choice, and the answer.
If music be the food of love, play on.*
**William Shakespeare**

We are born into this life like a blank canvas. We learn to survive through our parents and carers. Their influence on us as babies and children is so massively under rated. Little people rely on their elders to teach them how to be good humans. Unconditional love and boundaries are the key to creating conscious and confident human beings. We are literally a product of our upbringing and the patterns and behaviours of our parents and/or carers.

If we are fortunate enough to have parents who are consciously living life and think even a little differently to the masses, then you are very fortunate indeed. Alternatively, if your parents had a traumatic upbringing themselves, odds are that you may carry those generational traumas yourself. For example, some people have generations of family abuse to contend with. There may be no recognition in their mind that they are continuing the cycle of abuse. They may also have been raised to be fully dependent on their parents for everything, including validating and enabling their poor behaviour. The key here is, as adults, that we all have a choice. We can choose to acknowledge and change these habits and underlying patterns that we have learnt along our journey so far. And it is a choice. Should we choose to ignore the underlying traumas because they are too painful to face and work on, we run the risk of creating 'disease'. This impacts and manifests both physically and psychologically and can often literally kill us.

Unfortunately, a good number of us choose to blame external factors or chemical imbalances for our instability, thus reaching for more chemicals to fix it. Instead, we should first acknowledge there are issues and traumas within all of us to varying degrees. I have met and known people that are so unhappy and stressed within their deep traumas and internal dialogue, they manifest such dis-eases like shoulder, neck, back, knee pain, etc. Most of the time, people are unaware of the power the mind body connection within us. It's an area I strongly urge you to investigate and put it to the test yourself. I have done this many times as it sounded so 'out there' when I was first introduced to this way of thinking by friends in the 1990s. I also recall mum and dad always talking about similar things like 'what we think we become' and so on. I remember seeing a book in our family kitchen back in the 1970s or 80s called, *Think Yourself Slim* (re-published 1999). When I think of it now, the mind body connection concept seems to have been with me subconsciously for a long time.

Louise Hay's book, *You Can Heal Your Life* (1984) is an excellent guide to test and understand this. It identifies ailments, their probable cause, and affirmations that help change your inner dialogue and patterns. Another golden guide for conscious self-healing is *Your Body Is the Barometer to Your Soul: So be your own Doctor* (1994) by Annette Noontil. Both books have been instrumental in my healing and changing my thought processes and patterns. There are many more resources like these that can have a massive impact on your health, your life, and the way you view the world.

Another super powerful resource in self-healing is meditation. Meditation has truly been the one constant in my life for many years and I am so grateful I was introduced to it at a very early age in my final two years of high school. I didn't quite understand it, but I knew I enjoyed it. I can say beyond doubt it has saved my life on more than one occasion. Many people struggle with the concept of meditation and believe they must clear their thoughts and become enlightened immediately. This is not the case unless you become a monk and live in the mountains of Tibet and practise for years and years. In today's world, there are so many distractions to take us away from having any actual quality quiet time to ourselves. This is why meditation is even more important in our healing and living journey.

For those of you that would like to start this process, I suggest beginning with simple guided meditations in the morning and at night before bed. It is imperative to set yourself up for a good day every morning and let go of all the day's stressful

## It's Your Choice

thoughts at night. By allowing your mind to fully rest and reset before you go to sleep, it sets you up for a sweet and peaceful sleep and enabling a fresh start every morning. I have included two free meditations at the end of this book. Just scan the QR code and commit yourself to meditate every day. You will soon notice a change if you are consistent. As with becoming good at anything, consistency is the key. Of course, for those of you who want to dive deeper into the many benefits of meditation, there are many possibilities to hone this skill. For example, transcendental or Vedic Meditation is amazing and has been used for thousands of years.

There is an abundance of knowledge and resources readily available to us on many platforms, just waiting to give us guidance on whatever journey we are on. The biggest obstacle to finding the right path and solutions is to know where to look.

If you are a meditator, then there's your first port of call. If you can readily connect with nature and sit in stillness in your favourite natural area, answers will come. If you have a confidant or sage, they may guide you well. However, if you don't have access or know how to gain access to any of these avenues, then find yourself a new 'tribe' or community that are on the same journey and feel safe in the power of the collective positive mindset.

Failing these avenues, a good mindset coach, hypnotherapist, counsellor or therapist could be the answer for you. It is imperative to connect with your coach. There needs to be a strong sense of trust and being in the right space. This is where you must listen to your intuition and do not settle for anything less. One size does not fit all. This is about finding someone who will help guide you to do the hard work you need to do to clear old patterns, belief systems and anything else that is standing in your way to finding and growing into the beautiful human you already are. We all have everything we need within us; we just need to stop long enough to find it.

We have a purpose on this planet, and sometimes it takes quite a while to figure this out. This is why it is so important to surround yourself with positive people who will celebrate your successes just as much as you celebrate theirs. Know that there is always a way forward, but sometimes it just seems so damn hard to find the path. The first step is to choose a path and walk slowly, taking one step at a time. And know, with the right guidance, you can do this!

### It's Your Choice

Q: Do you have a favourite book that has inspired and helped you to grow/heal? Write it below or note a book or books you would like to read.

Date: _____

_____

_____

_____

_____

# CHAPTER 4

# My Defining Moments

*Every thought I think is creating my future.*
**Louise Hay**

Believe.

Believe in yourself, believe that you are in the right place. Even if you're in the middle of the biggest shitstorm of your life, you are in the right place. The incredible lessons we gain from the worst times of our lives make us find the path. It's true, some of us just seem to cruise through, looking like we've got it all sorted, the envy of so many. However, if you lift the veil, you'll find in most circumstances, they too are struggling with their inner selves.

Often, the people we think that have got it all sorted are some of the loneliest people on the planet. They get to a place where they may have made a lot of money, have fame, nice houses, cars, boats, etc. But their lives are often empty of anything real—they can't feel anything because they seemingly have everything. Their bucket appears full, but it's actually empty. They get so busy chasing and gaining they forget we are all here to help one another. Hence the hollow, shallow emptiness of this type of success. Many people, especially those in the spotlight, are looking for something to help them feel something, anything. This is where the gold is. It all comes from within. We cannot heal or feel from the outside. You cannot smell the ocean without breathing it in first. Hence, why so many turn to drugs, alcohol, and prescription drugs. They have forgotten that everything is within us. It is much easier to take something to make us feel better instantly instead of learning and doing the internal work to solve the cause of the pain. More on this later in the book.

# My Defining Moments

Let's now look at how we collect these scars that lead to disenchantment, disbelief, shame, anger, depression and all the pain that comes with trauma. For me, I count myself extremely fortunate to have had such a loving family base and adventure filled upbringing. Which always leads me to ask how the hell did I end up having to go through all the trauma that I did?

I have a few theories, but I will explore those in later chapters as well. For now, I will share my own significant scars and how they have been instrumental in my unwise choices of relationship partners. What does believing I could fly like Pippi Longstocking, pretending I was an acrobat in a circus, and falling off the monkey bars in primary school, getting knocked off my bike and having it stolen, getting cheated on by partners and being married and divorced three times have in common? The short answer is that they were all choices I made, thinking and believing they were right for me. Instead ultimately these choices created deep traumas and an accumulation of deep scars. On the flipside, they also created deep learnings.

Many times, along my journey I have questioned, why does this always happen to me? Why is it so damn hard for me to choose partners that are whole within themselves, and not just seeing the good in them and hope that I can bring out the best in them somehow? I know I'm not the only one who behaves this way, find a nice person who portrays themselves as confident and together for the first few years (some, way less) of the relationship, then all the sudden their exterior shell crumbles and they become 'wishy washy' and somehow forget they were in love with me. What I've learned since is that it was always my choice and specifically that it was not at all about them, it was all about me!

When I think about my relationships, especially as mentioned earlier, my first love was in high school. He was two years older than me, and I knew he was serious about our love and me. It certainly seemed and felt a lot longer than six months. It was wonderful. We had a great and beautiful courtship, and it led me to believe that this was the norm. It wasn't. The bar was set high and as I stumbled through my teenage years, I entered my first long-term relationship in my mid-teens and said no to sex for over a year, before I considered myself ready and mature enough. It was an interesting and eye opening experience, and I realise now how fortunate I was to have had such a respectful boyfriend. It opened a whole new world of fun and adventure. I found I loved making love. Who knew!

## My Defining Moments

We had a great time over the years we were together, except of course, the thing that ended it. This was my first cheating experience. I found out through a friend he had slept with someone else, and that was pretty much it for me. There were no excuses as far as I was concerned. It had run its course. I moved on quickly, via a casual 'friend with benefits', then into another long-term relationship with an old school friend. This time he was a little younger than me, and he was an incredible musician, and it was quite feisty and exciting. We had many ups and downs over our four years together, and I was quite smitten and held on tight. I fear it may have been too tight, or maybe I was just too young! Who knows, but once again came another cheat.

When confronted, both guys swore blindly that they hadn't cheated, but the truth always comes out, just like the sun and the moon. And even if it doesn't appear at first, know that it will, and know that in the long term, it doesn't matter. The damage has been done; more scars were collected. When someone allegedly cheats and is confronted, that fact that you're even discussing it in the first place just means that your partner is not who you thought they were. You then have the choice if their behaviour is acceptable to you? No matter what excuses they come up with. Choose wisely, is all I can advise.

## The Scars We Carry

I know a few women who have been cheated on and stayed in their relationship or marriage for many different reasons. To me, it feels like they have never really recovered from the betrayal, and it shows outwardly in their underlying sadness, their words, in their health and so on. Even though they may never acknowledge this, as it's been too long and become too enmeshed within them, they end up living as 'roommates' for the rest of their lives. It's sad to me, all that wasted time and potential for true love and happiness. Gone, just like that.

Think long and hard if you're in this situation. We all deserve to find our person, to love and be loved. The one that makes your heart sing and stomach do flips when they are near you or touch you in a certain way. The smile that stretches your lips so wide you think you're going to burst at the seams. Is this what you want to miss out on? I understand it though. It is tremendously difficult to trust when you've been hurt, especially more than once, twice, and the rest. It's hard when you don't trust your own intuition anymore, especially when you acknowledge it was screaming at you from within each time you made a wrong choice.

That was me, after surviving a violent and emotionally overpowering relationship. When I finally had the

## My Defining Moments

courage to seek help, to get out, and stay out, I realised I hadn't listened to my gut instinct, my higher self. And it had been screaming at me to stay away for a long time. But I'm skipping ahead a little.

As mentioned in the previous chapter, I met my first husband through the independent music scene in Brisbane. I'd seen him in his band several times before I finally met him. He was a bit of an enigma on the scene and was sexy and confident on stage. I guess you need to be when you're the lead singer. We started dating and eventually I moved in with him in a shared house. It was the best of times and so much fun. Living in your twenties truly is the most amazing time of your life. You're no longer a teenager and you're not quite a serious adult. Life is like a vast amusement park made for adventures and fun.

We spent countless nights at live music gigs, dinners, jazz bars, enjoying city life. We also enjoyed the great outdoors, bush walks, camping, surfing, beach holidays, skiing and weekends on our motorbikes. Living in Sweden for just under two years, travelling on our motorbike for three months around Europe, we also backpacked through Turkey, Greece, Italy and then north home to Sweden. The two long European adventures were amazing, so amazing. We even married in the Town Hall of my hometown, built in the 1500s, a stunningly beautiful piece of history.

We lived a classic city lifestyle, movies, restaurants, live music, including playing in a few bands. Returning to Australia from Europe, I settled into my new job, and he did the same. We bought and renovated a great apartment near a huge, beautiful park and river. It was a fantastic lifestyle, and all seemed to be well. However, there was always an underlying current of discontent, and gradually, the bond and closeness we once shared faded. My interests in self-development and spiritual growth outgrew our relationship. He didn't seem interested in that path and so things became strained, especially after the passing of a close friend and I fell into a heap. To me, it seemed he just didn't have the emotional tools to be there for me.

It occurred to me years later that this was the beginning of the end for me. Some months later my best friend was heading off on a seven-day wilderness trek in Tasmania. Her excitement was building and out of the blue, two weeks before her trip, I asked if I could come too. It caught both of us by surprise, and of course she was overjoyed with the idea. I was so excited and did not know what was in store for me, both physically and mentally. In my early

## My Defining Moments

thirties, I figured I was fit and healthy, and it didn't even register to me that trekking requires a different type of fitness.

I went through some challenging moments during our eighty-five-kilometre walk. We had to carry everything in and out, nothing was left behind. Once you entered the Overland Track, the only way out was at either end. We were fully committed. There was no turning back, come rain, hail, or snow. This was it.

During our little bush walk, some major shifts and realisations happened for both of us. I had never been on such a big hike ever and was totally in awe of the amazing landscapes and the absolute sheer beauty of this tiny part of the planet. As we walked the trails, they were tough and the physical, emotional, and mental pain was intense. I was fortunate to meet a man who practiced reiki about halfway. He literally saved my knees. My borrowed pack was so heavy, my feet were blistered, and everything hurt. But it was my knees that gave me the most grief.

He asked me, "What 'male' are you kneeling to?"

I immediately said, "What?"

It was my right knee that was really smashed —he told me the right side of your body refers to the masculine, hence the question. Anyhow, we chatted about all the meanings behind it, and it hit me like a train. I need to seriously look at my relationship and reconsider 'why' I was holding on so tight. He performed his magic, and when I got up, I had released so much—I didn't feel any pain or discomfort. Oh, my gosh, I had had no pain at all. The relief was immediate, and it left me wondering if I'd actually imagined the pain. Had I dreamt it? I was dancing and jumping with delight. I felt a twinge in my knee and thought I'd better stop pushing it, otherwise I'd undo all the energy release and likely create actual physiological damage!

My pain was better, but deep within, I knew I had major choices to face and decisions to make. We meandered through the rest of the trek and finally made it to the end at Lake St. Claire. Wow, seeing and feeling running water from a tap was winning like winning the lottery—it was amazing, and I won't mention what it was like to use a flushing toilet again. This was the late 1990s, there was nothing flash at all about this trek. We slept on wooden beds, cooked with our own mini stoves, collected water from nearby streams, and I had the most fantastic time of my life to date. It was so different from any day

## My Defining Moments

or overnight walk I had ever done. What's more are the incredible deep soul revelations I found. The vast and varied natural environments during the six days of hiking were visually and physically incredible. We walked in the pitch black of night, and me, totally unprepared, only had the smallest, useless torch you can imagine. I had only brought one torch for lighting the way to the amenities—not trying to find our way to the next hut! I remember thinking what can I distract myself with that would distract me from the fear I was feeling and how stupid could I be to bring such a useless torch! It's a great metaphor for making sure you are ready and prepared for difficult and challenging endeavours.

It truly was an epic adventure filled with life changing experiences and massive personal growth. Whenever I think of this adventure, I just want to go there and do it again and again. And I will, albeit with everything I need on such a quest, including and especially training for it properly. The pure solitude you can have out in the wilderness is a gift from nature. Go bush, you'll never regret it, but make sure you are fully fit and fully prepared, oh and pack lightly!

Back at home, I felt misplaced, and the internal unrest was too much to bear. I muddled through for months not knowing which way to turn or what to do. I had fleetingly heard and felt the cues for change, but buried them back deep down inside, back to where they were before. I returned to pretending everything was okay. We planned for and went on our annual migration to the snow, but this time we went to New Zealand to ski. It was fun and super challenging as it was super rocky, icy, steep—no trees anywhere to be seen. The ski field was on an actual volcano and many of the trails followed the volcano's historical lava and lahar flows. It had erupted 3–4 years earlier and you could still taste residual ash in the water in the hut we were staying in. Then disaster struck, or did it? I skidded on an icy patch, fell and smashed my hand and knew immediately it was broken. I had incurred a spiral break to the bone in my left hand, specifically my ring finger. Because of the immediate swelling, I had to remove my wedding ring and subsequently that ring was never worn again.

## My Defining Moments

Q: Have you knowingly made any significant choices or decisions that have created deep scars that you still carry?

Date: _____

_____

_____

_____

_____

_____

# CHAPTER 5

# Oh No, Not Again

*Everything I lose is found again, everything that is hurt is healed again.*
**Louise Hay**

Wow, that was the most life changing and pivotal experience I had ever had. I came back a totally different person. I felt the walls closing in and it felt as though the city buildings were all going to fall and crush me through the pavement. It felt like I was becoming agoraphobic, fearful of crowded places, and didn't want to leave home most days. I knew then I couldn't delay the inevitable any longer. I needed to change my life and soon. I ended my first marriage. It was the worst feeling and I hate that I caused such pain and hurt to my husband, I was the worst! I could no longer pretend everything was okay, so I went through six weeks of talking and trying to explain how and why I was feeling the way I was. It was torture. I had to go. After successfully applying for a year's leave of absence, I decided I needed to visit family and friends around the globe and got a one-way ticket around the world, starting in New Zealand.

As the trip around the world adventure began, I felt the release of so much as the plane gained momentum, speeding down the runway. The wheels lifted, and so did my spirits in the hopes of a fresh break and start. The heaviness and emotional upheaval of the past months faded as we flew higher and higher into the sky. There truly is no better feeling than physically removing yourself from your environment to create major shifts and change in your life.

I was picked up by a friend who had offered me lodgings. I felt an immediate spark, a deep connection and unfortunately did not have the sense to put any boundaries up. All I was thinking was I needed change. It didn't take long before we got together. In fact, that instant connection grew so deep, so quickly, my head and heart were spinning. I was convinced I'd found my soul mate, twin flame, the love of my life. Call it what you will, it's what I felt. In the short few months, I had planned to stay in New Zealand, we had an amazing time together. I helped renovate a house that he had bought in readiness for sale, in exchange for a roof over my head.

This 'love-ride' was fun and exciting, but it was fraught from the start, and I should have heeded the red flags that kept popping up. I wasn't over my marriage breakdown and hadn't even had time to process it yet. All I knew was I needed to bury the pain of it, and this was my way of dealing with it. Absolute denial was my answer. If I could go back in time and give myself a stern talking to I would! This was definitely one of the poorest choices I have made in my life. However, there was one beautiful thing to come from it, my daughter. Before too long into this new adventure, I found myself in tears over the way he spoke to and treated me. Everything was on his terms and when it suited him. I had wondered why he'd never been married at age forty. Hindsight is only a good teacher after you consciously wake from the heavy dream you're in. He would do just enough to keep me on the hook. Every time I wanted to leave, he wore me down with flowers, love cards, champagne, and (empty) promises.

I left to continue my world trip with an even heavier weight in my heart. I had left my marriage, jumped into another relationship, what the hell was I thinking? All I had now was my backpack filled with clothes, books, my compact disc player, and discs to keep me company on my journey. I flew into Los Angeles and was so ecstatic to see my friends there to pick me up. After a few days in LA, we flew up to their home in San Francisco, where I was fortunate to stay for a couple of weeks. I had an incredible time seeing the sites and playing the tourist. A day trip to Napa Valley wine country with my gorgeous friend, flying in a light aircraft and 'buzzing' the Golden Gate Bridge, Pier 39, Seal Rocks etc. Seeing San Francisco from the air is something that I am particularly grateful for.

Next stop was Chicago for a few weeks to spend time with my gorgeous friend who I'd worked with in Australia a few years back. We had a wonderful time exploring Chicago together, particularly the Blues Bars, the Adler Planetarium with her beautiful aunt, all the famous buildings, so much to see and do. The city of Chicago is beautiful, and I enjoyed every minute of my stay.

Next stop, New York, the Big Apple! Wow, just wow! I had never been to this side of the US before and was in complete awe of this incredible city. I was fortunate to stay in the Upper West Side with a friend's parents. New York is one of my absolute favourite cities in the world. It has everything you could ever wish for, the exhilarating vibe, the food, amazing people. I visited the Twin Towers, the Statue of Liberty, Central Park, Fifth Avenue, Times Square and so much more. It was astonishing, I have travelled to many cities, but this was something else. My friends from LA flew up to say hi, catch up and go out to dinner. This was my very first experience of having to wait to be seated for dinner for what seemed hours, even though we had a reservation.

I was amazed that amongst the noise, you can even find a peaceful spot to sit in stillness in this massive, bustling city. And as a lone traveller, I felt safe and loved every second I spent there and look forward to returning in the future. This is starting to sound like a travel blog, but bear with me it is all part of the journey and the collection of scars.

After New York, I visited Boston and stayed with another friend we'd met on that fateful Tasmanian hiking trip. Visiting Boston was a dream come true for me. To visit Harvard University, walk across the commons and just sit and breathe in all the sights, sounds and energy of this iconic university was outstanding. Another beautiful city with beautiful people, places, and food.

Then it was on to the United Kingdom to visit friends in London and Yorkshire.

As I remember this trip, I absolutely loved the feeling of being on my own and being fully present in my own space and power. No one telling what or how I should do things, making my own decisions in my own time. The memories as I write these words are so powerful. It inspires me for life, and living it to the full and reminds me how grateful I am for where I am now, and what is yet to come. And a huge reminder of my journey so far with all the lessons learned from people, events, challenges, and how it has shaped me and my personal growth. It confirms that we are all in fact in the right place, right now in accord with the choices and decisions we have made along the way.

## Oh No, Not Again

I will be forever grateful to all my beautiful family and friends across the globe for allowing me to come and stay with them and especially to my dear friend in the US, who at the time worked in the travel industry, guided me through my travels and was kind enough to upgrade many legs of my journey. This was an amazing gift which I will treasure forever. Unfortunately, this amazing adventure will also be overshadowed by the intensity of the man in New Zealand. He was emailing, and I was responding the whole time I was away. He treated me badly many times before I left and kept reeling me in with his charms and promises throughout the trip. I was absolutely besotted. I was totally under his spell. He somehow manipulated my thoughts, my feelings, and especially my fragile heart. It became all about him. I became absolutely entranced by him. When I think about it now, I am so disappointed and appalled with myself and how I could have allowed this craziness to enter my life!

Those of you who have ex-partners of the narcissistic persuasion and escaped will understand what I'm saying. The continual excuses you make to family and friends for their behaviour becomes part of your being. The gradual stripping of your self-esteem and self- worth, you actually start believing that somehow, it's your fault for everything that goes wrong for them. It is an impossible vortex of pain, pleasure, and adventure. Unfortunately, skewed more on the side of pain with the manipulation, abuse, and psychological torture. All the while, I convinced myself I had to maintain an outwardly happy life and pretend that everything is okay and it's only a phase, things will be different, better even, when... waiting for the 'when' and the promises never happen. Years go by very quickly in this vortex. You are fed little morsels of hope to keep you on the hook. You receive the lies of, "I promise I'll change; I promise I'll do better," with so much hope in your heart, you believe every word.

By the time you realise what is happening, you are so deep in it, there is no way to get out. Can you believe I left him once a year for five years? I physically moved out of our home, but I didn't move far enough away though. He stalked me every time, sent little enticing messages, presents, and promises of a beautiful life together. I got sucked in every time. We finally got married, had a baby girl, and that's when things went from bad to worse.

His threats became more and more menacing, and his violent tendencies became incredibly frightening. I remember so many times he towered over me with his black eyes (the colour they went every time he lost it, he even had tiny slithers of froth in the creases of his mouth) especially during my pregnancy. I remember running out of the house into the cold so afraid I would sit among the trees on the property, crying in desperation and hopelessness. It didn't get any better once my baby was born, as I was wishing it would. As he became even more obsessive and violent, I knew I had to save my baby girl and myself. The straw that broke the cycle for me was the second time he pinned me to the lounge by my throat, looked me in the eyes and said quietly, "I could kill you right now." I knew I had to get out! I have never felt terror like this in my whole life. I thought this is it, this is how I die!

I had reached out to a local service, The Smith Family, and they guided me through a process of getting out safely and permanently. My closest friends, who he'd alienated me from, dubbed it 'the great escape.' But this was only the beginning of my biggest challenges that were yet to materialise.

What ensued was to be the greatest heartache and uphill climb I have ever faced, and I certainly will not choose to participate in anything like it again in this lifetime. The pain and manipulation that my family and I had to endure for years as a consequence of one person. My belief is that we are all products of our upbringing, influences, and experiences. However, I also believe there is no excuse for this type of behaviour in adulthood, except by choice. We get to choose if we want to continue the cycle or break free from it. Saying that, I understand that unless you become consciously aware and take positive action to change, you will not be able or even understand that you 'need' to do something about it. This may be the result of parents, guardians or loved ones who condone and 'enable' the poor behaviour to consciously, or unconsciously, validate their own trauma related behaviours.

He continued the behaviour with a vengeance, particularly with his own child, and even using her as a pawn from the very moment I fell pregnant. It was a surreal situation to be in, having come from a family of openness, support, and encouragement to become an independent human being. I found myself in a situation that I did not know how I ended up in. What the hell? How was I ever going to negotiate this psychological abuse, dodge the physical abuse, keep my child safe and live to tell the tale? I had fallen in love so hard with what now feels like a 'monster', and I was exposing my child to this! I had to find a way out.

## Oh No, Not Again

The first port of call was to talk with someone who could help me make some sense of the situation. I felt like I was trapped in an endless nightmare and that I was losing my mind. I fully believed I was going crazy and my self-worth and self-esteem were sub-zero. I'd never experienced it before and did not know where to go or what to do. I felt embarrassed, ashamed, and too scared to talk about it. I had no voice left after being told time and time again, "it's my word against yours and who is going to believe you anyway?" Even writing these words sends shivers down my spine. I felt so lost and alone.

A very perceptive nurse who was doing the fifteen-month health check for my daughter could see through the blurred crusade I was on, and asked, "what is actually going on?" My guard came down for the first time, and the words and tears flowed. It was the wake up call and release from the years of freeze-fight-or-flight living. Living only in a constant state of survival, I didn't even realise I was so deeply entrenched in it. I am so grateful for this beautiful ray of human light. I truly believe she saved both my daughter and me.

This was the beginning of the end of this toxic, demented relationship. I went through counselling, many discussions with my doctor and finally had the nerve to reach out to a friend for help to get out. I felt riddled with guilt that I was responsible for the whole thing, that it was my fault. He did such a number on me. It took years of self-help books, self-help programs, domestic violence counselling, and thousands of hours of meditation to navigate my back to a somewhat stable state of mind. Every minute of this long journey was worth the blood, sweat, and tears to find my happy self, my self-esteem, and build my self-worth once again. I'm still not sure how I functioned in my full-time job, looked after my daughter, and stayed afloat. All I knew was that I had to look after my daughter.

The first court papers were date stamped and arrived on my daughter's second birthday. Was this a cruel joke? It was the first of many legal affidavits with his lies and allegations about me being a perpetrator and that he was 'afraid' of me. Unfortunately, the court system was not geared up to look after victims of domestic violence and they certainly, in my experience, did not put the children's best interest first. There is an appalling number of women and children that have been abused and killed by unstable partners, parents and family members. There appears to be nothing done to properly address this. I am dumbstruck at how this still occurs today.

## Oh No, Not Again

Despite the drawn-out court process, which is the case in many countries, it did not seem to mean anything, anyway. He was found guilty of domestic violence towards both me and my daughter, and I mistakenly thought that meant that it would offer protection. The following year, he was rewarded with fifty percent custody. In my diagnosed PTSD mind I thought, custody to potentially manipulate, brainwash, groom, and control. We went through fourteen years of hell and bound by the court order that forced the 'week about' torment of my child. Each week, she came home it took up to five days for her to relax and be herself, then it was time to go back.

My heart broke every single Friday when I had to say goodbye knowing she may be manipulated, told lies and controlled by someone she trusted and loved. It was the worst. Thankfully, my daughter was resilient and also clever to realise something was not right, and made the decision to move home to us and away from him.

Unconditional love, freedom of choice and independence are what our children need to know as they are growing and moving into adulthood. Not pressure to perform like seals, or to do things their parents didn't get to do or achieve when they were young. They need boundaries as children, good strong guidance as teenagers, an abundance of unconditional love and support always.

I am grateful everday to my parents who had the incredible foresight to teach me to be so independent and and have the courage to follow my dreams. It has been invaluable. Having lived in several countries, my parents valued their own independence and freedom of choice. Hence their deep love for Australia, the absolute freedom, the wildness of the land and the multicultural landscape of people that live within it.

Mum always taught me to be kind and accepting of people no matter where they came from or who they appeared to be. "People are people, we are all just people," she said. This rings home and is true to me now more than ever, knowing that we are all connected as a species on this planet. It doesn't matter if we come from opposite ends of the globe, we are all affected by climate, storms, earthquakes, wars, etc. When mother nature kicks back in a big way, we all suffer. Mum used to say whenever another 'natural' disaster occurred, it was mother nature shaking off some excess 'fleas' from her back.

## Oh No, Not Again

The advent of global connectedness via technology allows us to understand that the old ways of 'boundary thinking' is archaic and caveman like. There are no more frontiers that haven't been explored, except perhaps the deepest depths of the oceans. Goodness knows what lies down there.

The sooner we acknowledge that we do not need to carry any of the burdens of our parents, and grandparents, forefathers and foremothers, the sooner we can find our true selves and let go of all the bullshit that creates so much anxiety, fear, depression and so on. We have a choice to be conscious about what and how we think, and what we tell ourselves. The term 'your word is your wand' is a great example of how we can destroy everything inside us by telling ourselves what and who we are. When you continually repeat 'I'm depressed'—you will be depressed! 'I am anxious'—you will be anxious! It's that simple, but it's also that hard! Or is it? Conscious reprogramming/rewiring is like changing an ingrained habit—it can take 18–254 days to create a new habit (Phillipa Lally, European Journal of Social Psychology 2009). This study found that, on average, it takes 66 days to form a new behaviour and for it to become automatic. The time it takes is likely to depend on the person changing and creating a new routine one step at a time is imperative. Like with anything new, there will be a period of adjustment and it will be very uncomfortable to even start.

For me, listening consciously to my own thoughts and internal conversations has become a game of sorts. I often think, what are you trying to sell me today? When I feel like crap and start to let my thoughts run away, I generally can catch them and swiftly kick it to the curb and create a positive pattern of thinking and talking to myself instead. It requires conscious effort and practice, but once mastered, you become exactly who you already are—a beautiful human being. You simply choose to NOT be a stupid human, thinking stupid things. It is very challenging and sometimes I choose just to let it be, let those thoughts race. I know they will pass and I'll come out the other side knowing I've either learned something I needed or they were just random thoughts. Some days are harder than others to stay on track, but please persevere. It is worth the discomfort.

Q: What negative thoughts are on 'repeat' in your mind?

Date: _____

_____

_____

_____

_____

_____

# CHAPTER 6

# The Vortex

*I am happy, calm and peaceful inside.*
**Louise Hay**

I now, more than I ever have before in my life, believe that all our lives are meant to evolve, but it can and will only happen if we choose it to. We evolve each time we feel uncomfortable in our own skin. The more discomfort we feel, the more we grow. However, we will not grow if we bury the feelings and revert to our comfort zones. The key here is to make a conscious choice to do something that absolutely scares the bejesus out of you. There is a reason we encounter these pivotal points of discomfort, pain, and trauma. They are 'messages' that something is not right in our life and we need to find out what the message is and choose to change or take a different path. Some may take the route of a tortoise and hide themselves within the safety of their shells, and some will squirm at the mere thought of doing something new. Choose to consciously lean into the discomfort and evolve. Each to their own, I have always said, but I truly believe there is no time left to stubbornly dig your heels in and pretend like everything is fine. It's not.

Changing the world only requires three and a half percent of the earth's population to effect major shifts in the larger population (as cited by David Robson, in an Article for the BBC, 2019), so come on, here's your invitation. Let's do it for ourselves, our children, loved ones and our communities. All we need to do is shift our thinking from negative to positive and watch how your world changes for the better.

Bob Proctor, RIP, identifies this so clearly in his amazing Abundance Meditation (found in the *Mindvalley* mobile App, the internet and You Tube), where he states, "The only limit in our own life is the

## The Vortex

limit in our own thinking, the limit that we place on our imagination…man's chief delusion is his conviction that there are causes other than his own state of consciousness. All that befalls a person, all that is done by him, all that comes from him, happens as a result of his state of consciousness… understand anything you can see on the screen of your mind; you can manifest in your material world. If you can hold it in your head, you can hold it in your hand…"

This meditation was always one of my go-to favourites, no matter what was happening in my world. It never failed to put me on the right path to conscious living and manifesting. Try it, see if it resonates. It definitely helped me and I listened to this one at least once every day. It's great to listen before you get up in the morning and again before you sleep at night. It was the destroyer of my negative self-talk and can be a great wakeup call for many.

As a collective, we need to make a shift from competing with one another and learn to work and have fun together if we are to survive as a species. We need to heal ourselves to heal our relationships on a personal and global level. This will ultimately heal the world and the mess it's been in for a long, long time.

It's interesting when I look back at my journey and I wonder, how many times do I need to heal myself, and when will the challenges ever stop? After negotiating the escape from the previous toxic relationship, I once again found myself in a different type of turmoil!

Have you ever felt so let down, so disappointed, and so hurt by someone that you absolutely trusted wholeheartedly for such a long time? Then to find out that trust has been broken. The trust that was absolutely unshakable. The amount of hurt and self-doubt it caused was significant. I was gobsmacked and it felt surreal. I know so many people go through this. And to be honest, this is the most pain, emotionally that I had ever been in. I had lost both parents within a few years, been abused and manipulated, suffered PTSD (post traumatic stress disorder) and depression, suicidal intentions, this speed bump was huge for me. In addition, I had to start all over again, in my late fifties.

It was so daunting to be in this situation. But thankfully, I had grown enough to know I had choices. I could choose to either face it head on and move through the shit one step at a time. Or I could lose myself and bury myself back in the pit of

# The Vortex

depression and sorrow. That familiar hole was calling my name. That old deep, cold, dark and narrow well-like hole with no way out! Holding on to the rhetoric of feeling sorry for myself, making 'woe is me' excuses, playing the victim, and my brain sinking into dark and frightening thoughts. Thankfully, the last time I was in there, I was conscious enough to leave a ladder and could climb out, one rung at a time. Though, I fell back in a few times—it's how the brain works, but I have learnt so much about the subconscious mind through my hypnotherapy training, I knew it was just trying to trick me back into the familiar patterns of behaviour.

Now, I know it's okay to feel down and acknowledge and pay respect to what has happened in the past and all the emotions that come with it. But now I choose to only visit this space for a little while and above all, I do not move back in there! I've learned to be consciously aware of my thought patterns and that my subconscious mind is just trying to look after me by going back into the familiar, the known. I unequivocally know that I am in control of my thoughts and how to steer away from the misguided belief that I have no control. I know how easy it is to make excuses and get sucked back into the vortex of self-sabotage and self-loathing. I know it is so much harder to face your demons head on. It takes work and can get pretty ugly!

For me, being on anti-depressants (or the like) is not an option. This is my choice. Years ago, in my twenties, I was prescribed them by a clinical psychologist. I justified it to myself because I had been diagnosed/labelled as having 'chemical imbalance' issues in my brain. I attached myself to that 'fact' because I was told by a professional that something was wrong with me and at the time it felt good to find out there was something 'wrong' with me. As time passed, I queried—how could she know there was a chemical imbalance? She couldn't measure it? Now, when I recall this time, I remember being stuck in a situation that I didn't want to be in. On a conscious level it gave me relief from this situation, but if I'd known more about the sub-conscious mind, I would have made a different decision, and instead of going on anti-depressants, I would have changed my situation and environment to test if that was the cause instead of a chemical imbalance. Perhaps there would have been no need for drugs to 'numb' the emotional discomfort I was feeling?

As a result, to appease my inquiring mind, I read countless books, meditated regularly, and used more holistic, naturopathic methods of tackling my physical and psychological challenges. I started to take notice of when I became ill. I was working in high stress corporate positions in the 1990s, I recognised a pattern. Each time I fell ill with some sickness, I recall consciously thinking, I really need a rest. But I wouldn't rest because I felt guilty for taking time off without being physically sick. Subsequently, out of nowhere, within days I would become ill and be out for the count with a cold or flu, sometimes for days. When I realised it could be me that created the illness, I put it to the test on numerous occasions. It worked every time. It became a game. This was a big learning and major discovery for me on the power of the connection of the mind and body.

In recent years, I have become acutely aware of so many things being labelled these days—and I ask, *why? Why do we need to label everything? For what purpose?* I question whether it creates a conscious and/or subconscious attachment to that label, making it okay to submit to it? Does it create the reason or justification for why we feel, do, or are a certain way? Is it a way for us to escape our current situation?

As mentioned earlier, I have been an avid fan of the mind body connection for many years and subscribe to finding the root cause of an ailment before diving into pharmaceuticals. I believe there is definitely a place for them, particularly in acute or life-threatening situations. I have been consciously connecting the mind body 'dots' since the nineties and have learnt much through experimenting on a personal level. There have been many psychological and subsequent physiological challenges for me over the last twenty-five years. I was a great test dummy and had lots to work with and test on myself.

The way we live life is a choice. No matter what situation we find ourselves in, there is an opportunity for change, specifically within our thoughts. This is where it all starts. We can begin to 'seed' new ways and solutions within our thoughts. If we follow certain protocols and methods, this will ultimately change our direction and life. Unless, of course, we find ourselves in a dire place of no return by having left it for far too long and ignored the cues and messages from within. You know your gut instinct. We can also choose to stay safe and live our lives as we have always done, hence giving little or no opportunity for growth and evolution, which is totally ok too. As a result, we may choose to live the way our society or religion has told us for hundreds of years, according to their rules and regulations.

## The Vortex

I was brought up to do the right thing, be polite and kind, assimilate as an immigrant in the early 1970s, respect my elders, use table manners and so on. It was frowned upon if we dared be different or not conform. I was brought up with strict rules and boundaries that kept me safe. Thankfully, my parents also taught me how to think for myself and adapt to change pretty quick if I did stray from the rules. In addition to the strict boundaries, I felt free to test and push them and was prepared for the consequences. My dad was always teaching me practical things, like car maintenance, woodwork and how to use my brain to fix things. I was taught about open communication, unconditional love and support, no matter what. Also, and this was a big one for me, that we all deserve to be loved and respected no matter who we are or where we come from, and that the world is our oyster if we choose.

When we are faced with significant adverse situations and slide into victim mode, our system often gets caught in the fight/freeze/flee/survive at all costs response. This often forces us to disappear within ourselves and it's easy to understand how our mental health deteriorates within our thoughts and bodies. It's so unconscious, most times we don't even notice it and we spiral into a vortex of negativity, sadness, and depression. The key here is to become super vigilant on where your thoughts are going, and to head them off at the pass before they really do your head in. Only you can choose to control this with practice and patience. Do your absolute best to stay conscious of your thoughts and internal dialogue. To live from the heart and a place of love, integrity, facing the real, versus perceived, fear you need to tap into that inner knowing that everything will be okay. I have found that it is imperative to connect first to your heart, then gently connect your heart to your head and things become so much clearer and so much easier. But 'wait, what, how', I hear you ask. This will be explored further in Chapter 9.

It takes clarity and courage to see and feel the surrounding opportunities. And if you are in a situation where you can't do that, reach out to someone that can help you to see them. Someone that can help guide you through so that you can see the potential pathways to more clarity and calm. Open your mind and know there is always a way out and forward. So many people get stuck in the detail. You may have heard of the saying, "the devil is in the detail." It is so important to go through a process to find your true self again and get on track, one step at a time. I know how these situations can be so overwhelming, and I know how hard it is to see a path forward. Trust me. The answer is to get some trusted guidance. Someone always knows someone who can help. Whether it be a close friend, family member, coach, counsellor or other worthy source. Also, know if you don't gel with someone, you don't have to stick with it, ask for a referral. It is imperative to have full confidence and trust in your guide. You are in charge and have the choice. Do not get bullied into anything that feels wrong. Listen to your gut. If like me, you have lost trust in your own gut, seek out a trusted family member or friend. You are not alone in this.

Seeking help was a huge one for me. Because I've always been very, very independent. I've always trusted myself to know what was best. Though, as I've experienced time and time again in my life, I made some very poor choices along the way and ended up in some shitty situations, which, in hindsight, I'd rather not have. Saying this, I also know that they have shaped me into the person I am and have clarified my purpose in this lifetime. I've always believed things happen for a reason and there is no failure, only fuel, lessons or knowledge. I still love Einstein's theory, "Insanity is doing the same thing over and over, expecting a different outcome." Whilst I know this has been discussed by scientists and philosophers over the years, it still rings true in circumstances where we find ourselves in an infinite negative loop. We need to understand we can step out of the loop and into new possibilities. Nothing changes, if nothing changes.

Choose to change. No one can do it for you. Sometimes you have to hear it repeatedly, sometimes for years, to finally hear it. I know so many things and situations I have consciously and unconsciously put myself through, not realising that I am responsible for that because I stayed in the loop. The loop becomes a kind of safety or comfort zone because you know what you'll get. It's the perceived fear of the unknown that keeps us in the loop. The mere thought of stepping outside of this can be insanely daunting.

If you're in that loopy situation, you really need to stop, look around, step outside and observe yourself, your thoughts, your patterns of behaviour and so on. Make notes, collect data. This can also be referred to as journaling. Do your research and start recognising your repeating patterns, sayings like, "it's just who I am," "I can't change who I am," etc and allow yourself the huge prize of finding your path to freedom and happiness. It is an inside job. Ask for help when you need to. The most important thing here is to be

## The Vortex

brutally honest with yourself and gently with those around you. Stop telling yourself bullshit stories. All it does is delay your own release to happiness and freedom. After all, isn't that what we all want? Freedom to just be our real selves without fear of judgment and worrying about what others think of us. Being with family, friends and loved ones who know, love and accept us, warts and all. It is the most amazing feeling to live like this. On the flip side, if you don't need any assistance, just know that you have the power within to make really good choices. To be free of the loopy 'vortex' of going round and round and round, spinning out of control at the mercy of everything and everyone outside you. Continuously wondering why you attract the same type of partner, why your partner it horrible to you, why life is treating you so badly and so on. Know that it is ultimately your choice to stay there, and it's also your choice to step out of this vortex.

Q: Are you stuck in a 'loop'? Note it down below and what can you do to change it?

Date: _____

_____

_____

_____

_____

## CHAPTER 7

# The Freshest Scars

*I am not defined by my past;
I am defined by my choices.*

To capture how easy it is to get stuck in the vortex. I will share the most recent scar I collected. It's hard to know where to begin and end this one. It was the most challenging few years of my life so far, and as you now know, my life has had a very colourful palette of challenges! Before I begin this chapter, I wish to say that this is wholly from my point of view it was how I experienced the situation and how I felt at the time.

## The Scars We Carry

My ex-husband did what I consider foolish, hurtful and unforgivable. It was so out of character for him and so hard to believe. It is said that time heals and after much reflection, I have a much clearer understanding of why things went the way they did, but at the time, it was just so inconceivable and painful.

Strike three, you're outta there! Was the thought that went through my mind when the divorce order for my third marriage came through. *I've done my dash, screwed the pooch. I'm doomed to fail at relationships,* on and on the internal dialogue went. I kind of laugh at these thoughts now, as I can see and acknowledge there had been an underlying river of dismay and denial about our future desires. Despite the heartfelt promises and assurances, we didn't seem to be on the same path into the future. When we married, I was convinced I had got it right this time, 'third time lucky'. Though, to be honest, shortly before the wedding, I saw a side of him that made the hairs on the back of my neck stick up. RED FLAG! I immediately deferred to my old pattern of making excuses. He's just tired, stressed from work. My excuses came thick and fast. I ignored the flag and instead listened to words in my head. Everything was already organised and set for our wedding and after all, he was just stressed. I didn't even question it.

## The Freshest Scars

I kept the torrent of my insecurity that was pulsing beneath the surface of our relationship well buried for many years, hoping things would change and get better and go back to the way it had been the first few years. After all, we loved each other and could get through anything right? It was 'happy days'. We were safe, our family had grown by one, our house renovations were complete, and all was well. Then, as life does, curve ball after curve ball hit. My beloved parents both passed away within a few years of each other, and set me back way more than I acknowledged at the time, trying to be strong and resilient for my family. My dream of us all moving home to Australia seemed to get further and further away. We started to drift apart and became less and less connected. It was hard to communicate on a deeper level.

I muddled through the grieving process of losing my parents, being away from my siblings and family in Sweden, I kept going, trying to hold myself together. The continued stress of court hearings, manipulation and other crap created by the previous ex in his bid to make my life as miserable as possible for leaving him. I found myself falling deeper and deeper into a massive and narrow pit of depression and despair. I did everything within my power to focus on the happy things in my life: my kids, my family, my beautiful in-laws, friends, and hobbies. I ventured into the realm of self-growth and learning new things and new ways so I could get myself through the boggy mire. Each time I felt I was moving forward and gaining some clarity, something knocked me and there was a compounding effect of darkness and despair.

I have since realised that I was, for years, concurrently going through that wonderful part of womanhood called menopause. It is no wonder that the menopause journey, coupled with the rest of my challenges, threw me into a complete state of flux. I have realised since how menopause also played a part in how I was feeling and thinking. I felt so lost and felt I no longer had any say in what was happening in my life. I am sad to say that on two occasions I was so close to the edge that I almost 'checked out' for good. I felt there was no way out and no way through. I was no good to anyone and everyone would be much better off without me. This was the rhetoric and dialogue on repeat in my mind. I was ready to bail out. It was so close, but something, somehow a faint voice or divine guidance, whatever it was, talked me out of it. I am forever grateful I didn't end it.

Sadly, I see how marred this way of thinking is, and it's given me a much greater understanding why so

## The Freshest Scars

many lose this battle and their life through suicide. It brings me to tears every time I think of how tragic it truly is, and I wish I could somehow bring clarity to them, and their loved ones left behind. *If this is affecting you in any way, please reach out to someone or call your local organisation that can and will help you.*

Thankfully, my husband was a great rescuer in the times of crisis and after my, let's call them 'blips', supported me and talked me through them. However, I knew deep down he couldn't rescue me from myself. I knew ONLY I could do that. The second time my thoughts and inner dialogue almost got the better of me, was the defining moment. The moment where I had scared myself so much with my thoughts and intentions, it shook me to my core and woke me up. I finally heard my good inner voice, or whatever it was, much louder this time and knew I had to do something, but what? This time, I dived in head first and deeper into meditation than ever before, watched webinars, read self-help books, listened to recordings and did myriad of self-development courses, and even took music lessons. I was on a desperate quest to find myself again and climb out of the deep hole of depression.

I found my solace in meditation and practiced several times a day and especially during the sleepless nights.

Of note and in particular, my go to meditations were by Tom Cronin, Vishen Lakhiani, Bob Proctor, Marissa Peer among many others. In fact, I purchased Marissa Peer's 'Free Yourself from Depression and Anxiety' recording, which I listened to at least once or twice per day for three months solid. This was the key to releasing my depression. I had seen many councillors, psychiatrists the preceding years for my PTSD. I was fatigued and desperate for deeper healing and change. The hypnosis, coupled with the meditations and daily actions, allowed me to once again find myself.

There seemed to be a light coming into view, and things started to be better.

I felt myself feeling more grounded and was moving in the right direction and hope came back into my being. We even moved forward with the plan to move to Australia and had purchased a property. A resignation letter had been written. We were all set to go. However, that plan was put on hold. For a good reason this time.

After fourteen years, the Court Order that held us captive and dictated our daily life finally dissolved and I could finally start to see freedom becoming real.

I felt myself have breakthrough after breakthrough and with the support of my husband, family, daily meditation and more counselling, I regained my self-worth, confidence, and had the courage to step back into my true self again. We had planned to move to Australia from the get-go and had bought a home that we would eventually move into. Things were really coming together—my daughter was home full time, and it was fabulous to finally be free of all the shackles and restrictions imposed by the Court Order and move forward with our lives.

Then COVID arrived with a massive shunt that put the world on hold. Shit! We were in the process of setting up our home in Australia and had plans to move in time for my daughter to finish high school, and our son to start high school in Australia. The ensuing obstacles came and went. My son and I moved to Australia, and my husband and daughter stayed behind whilst she finished high school. The prolonged shut down of New Zealand played havoc with being able to see each other, but once the border openings were announced, my husband was booked and flew over immediately. I was so excited but stressed to the max, worried about whether he would like our new home, where we lived, and so on.

After a few days, he said he totally understood why I was so happy and loved living in the area we had chosen. I finally relaxed, let go of my worries and was so looking forward to us all being together as a family again, starting fresh and starting a new adventure.

A few months after his next visit, things changed and took a drastic turn for the worse. I was ghosted. There were no one to one calls or even contact outside the routine 'family' chats. Then finally, I mustered the courage to call and ask what was happening. We talked, but nothing real and, from my point of view, truthful came from it. Finally, he suggested couples counselling, to which I immediately agreed, and three months later, it was blindingly obvious to me he was not interested in trying to make it work. Every option I put forward was pushed back. I said openly in one of the final sessions, after giving in, "it's obvious that your heart is not with me, it's with someone or something else." I did not know at the time he had not been honest for eight months about where he'd been and what he'd been doing. It turned out to be inconsequential, but at the time it was not.

The rollercoaster ride of pain, anxiety, grief, and the cumulative emotional torment of previous years took its toll once again. He made the choice to change paths, and I fully acknowledge we are all entitled to change our minds. It was then up to me to choose to accept that and move on with my path. I was at the end of my rope, I felt I'd reached my limits. So, I sent an email with some sensitive questions, I was back in peak stress mode. We even spoke a few times that gave me hope, I even felt we could reconcile and move through it. Gratefully, since then we have worked through the mire and continue to this day to maintain a good relationship.

However, at the time this was all happening, this is where my mind went:

*The whirlwind of thoughts, feelings and incredible sadness became all too much and I once again exploded into tears. Sign on the dotted line, make promises to be kind and respectful and think of the children and their best interests. How can I move forward when there is no light? How can I move forward when I can't even see my feet? Swept away from under me, I buckled and folded like a card of old. When will this torment end? When will I stop this pretend and get real? Finally, admit to myself, the only person I can rely on is me.*

*I need to stop putting my own heart and life on the line for others when deep down I know this person is not one* hundred percent for or with me. I need to realise they have not 'seen' the real me and that's my bad for not acknowledging or noticing this sooner. However, saying that we can only make decisions with the knowledge we have at the time. The fact is, I fully believed in him and that he was with me 100%.

My mind is aghast at all that has passed. Once again it's been a farce! The straw has been drawn and the camel's back is totally worn, and there is no more strength to carry anything.

Filled with sadness and no tomorrows. IT'S NOT FAIR!! My heart screams, whatever happened to all our dreams. Dreams of fun and adventures to places new and places old. Flying free together so beautiful and so bold. And now for the sake of someone ex, it's turned the whole thing quite complex.

What of love, what of commitment, and what of us? You've gone and thrown everything under a bus. Smashed, trashed and obliterated, there is my heart, or a small piece of it. Where is the rest? I'll have to go on a journey to find my shattered and scattered heart—like finding a mirror in a million tiny pieces.

### The Freshest Scars

*It'll take some time to find them all I know, but find them I will and put them in a backpack as I go. Once I have them, I will journey home to do my best to build and repair the broken pieces that once was my heart. I will see myself in the mirror again.*

*How can anyone do this, cause so much pain and destruction? You have no right, no privilege, no instruction, to do as you have and then throw it back to me, like it was my fault. I was clear and true from the start of what was in mind and in my heart, there was nothing but honesty, love and belief. You promised, you assured me, and we all agreed. The family plan was decreed.*

*It is now clear there was no intention or will to 'fight for me or us'. How could you just aim so directly for the bus?*

*Now that all is said and done, I feel sad for you and what you've become. The mistruths and secrets that seem to easily flow, but what was behind the scenes, I did not know. Time will heal my shattered heart. The pain and hurt will also brew, but man oh man, this scar will be huge.*

*And what of the learnings from this episode, this novel of our lives together? I guess I can only take a step forward when I'm able. All I know now is that I'm at a new table! And you are not.*

It was sink or swim time, again. It was time to dig the deepest I've ever dug and find my inner Captain Marvel, soak up all the energy and power I could muster and move graciously and fearlessly into the future. But first, I had to face the shitty truth and negotiate my extraction from this web of uncertainty, misconception, and untruths. The 'pre-tend' must end and accept the fact that I want everything! I want and deserve a love story of unconditional love, trust and being with 'my' person. The person who loves me, not the thought of me, not what they think I should be and what they want me to be. I am finally awake to who I need in my life to walk beside me and just want me for me. IT'S ME!

During this incredibly difficult time, I had to go for a colonoscopy (then, subsequently, another two). In my thoughts, I knew I had been dealing with so much 'shit' and accepted it for so long and it literally manifested itself in my colon! I waited for the results for what seemed like an age. Thankfully, the results were benign, but I had a significant number of large polyps that had to be removed. This is something I continue to monitor every year, and strongly urge

## The Freshest Scars

anyone over fifty to do 'the poo test'. I am without doubt, this was the wake up call I needed and another life lesson to pack in my kit bag.

As I negotiated my hurt and trauma, I can sincerely say I could put my hand on my heart and feel the pain pulsing. From one minute to the next, I didn't know whether to laugh, scream or fall into a heap and cry a waterfall of tears. All I know is it hurt so damn much and I knew I could either choose to be consumed by it and get sick (i.e. opt out) or choose to feel into every second of it and use it to strengthen my resolve to learn and grow from it and use in service to help people who also want to get better and move into a more positive life. It ended up being a no-brainer choice for me, but it took a long time to move through it. In fact, anger, sadness, fear and frustration continue to rear their ugly heads and I stay vigilant with my thoughts and just 'visit' with them for a bit, acknowledge them and let them go with love and light. I know if I don't continue to do this, I will be so consumed, overwhelmed and sucked back into the vortex again. We all know that doesn't bode well for anyone, especially me.

I know that when I eventually come to be with someone new, I know they need to have the willingness and ability to journey through life, growing together and separately on the same path. No bullshit reasons why it won't work, why this or why that. There is only YES, and let's work out how together. I need a doer and a positive soul to love me for me and have the ability to stretch each other so we can safely, lovingly and confidently move forward together.

Who wants to be with the wrong person for the wrong reasons? Who wants to be in a relationship always wondering if it's right? Why waste your life pretending and moving forward towards to your dreams, only to have someone not feel the same? I have pretended and believed with my whole heart thinking I was on the right track, but deep-down feeling there was something not quite right. The eternal optimist in me kept saying it was close enough, so it would work. I know now that pretence, 'close enough' and all the wishing in the world won't change its course and it will ultimately catch you out. This is where everything comes unstuck on the inside and the outside. You can choose to ignore what you know deep inside, and keep pretending, or you can choose to go on the road not travelled and take a chance on you. You never know, one day you may just find that 'your person' is looking for you too.

## The Freshest Scars

My person, what even is that? Does it even exist? I wonder, and yes, I do believe it exists and I will find him when I am the real me and stop making excuses for men and their poor behaviour. I do not want to be with anyone who cannot see the beauty in all people, even behind the facades they may carry and we all have facades. I have learnt this through my life journey, and as mum always said, "people are just people, we all come from the same place." Deep down I'm convinced we are all looking for a life of fun, love and peace.

There is no place in this life anymore for bullshitters, cads, misogynists, pretenders, judgmental, hypocritical arseholes. Particularly those who blame everyone and everything for their own shortcomings.

"Oh my god! Just grow a pair and get on with it!" Is what I would normally say, but I understand, they too have a history and reason for their own insecurities and behaviour patterns. There is an innate need to justify what they are feeling inside and projecting it to those who are usually nearest to them. As Vishen Lakhiani says, "…hurt people, hurt people."

My parents were way ahead on so many levels, definitely not perfect, but I will be forever grateful to them. They had what I believe is a real relationship. They had deep love for each other, but they also knew communication was key and sometimes that communication got loud. To give you an insight into what my 'normal' was, dinners were always at 5pm and everything was open for discussion—the good, bad and ugly—it was very open and everything discussed.

I felt somewhat robbed of my opportunity for this closeness to continue with my own family. In addition the ongoing challenges we faced for such a long time with the Court Ordered parenting regime, it was fraught with the constant badgering and uncertainty. I spent years defending and deflecting incoming bombs from the second ex husband. Despite being constantly stressed and in survival mode, I did absolutely everything I could to maintain some semblance of a quality family life. Throughout this time, I had to be hyper vigilant with my thoughts and not let my old patterns take over, but sometimes things got through, and I had to pull myself up.

I have spoken with many mothers over the years who've negotiated separation and divorce, it is particularly devastating those who have been in controlling relationships. Unfortunately, I have known some that gave up the fight and their lives as a result.

## The Freshest Scars

If you are in a relationship with a person who is not congruent with who you are—and one or both of you do not see the value in adapting, or compromising to work it out together, it will catch up. It becomes incredibly difficult to even look at one another, the connection is lost, resentment builds, and you can no longer be your true self. The vicious cycle of pretence and defence begins. Also known as people pleasing, not rocking the boat, unable to speak one's own truth, you lose yourself, your self-worth and self-esteem and you feel bad, even guilty for bringing things up that your partner doesn't want to talk about. The disconnect gets wider and wider as time goes by. Finally, you're at your wits' end and must do something, but what?

Q: What behaviours have you accepted from your partner in the past? Is there a different way you would like to connect?

Date: _____

_____

_____

_____

_____

_____

# CHAPTER 8

# The Cracks Appear

*If you don't know how to say no, your body will say it for you through physical illness.*
**Gabor Mate**

When we arrive in the place of feeling totally lost and wondering *how the hell did I get here*, we have no clue or recollection of how we got in the mess we're in. It's quite frightening and like we've been on autopilot for goodness knows how long. In my circumstances, it was because I totally forgot how important I am and that I matter too. I was busy being everything to everyone else. I forgot me! Everyone will have their own story, reason and circumstances, but it comes down to how easy it is to lose ourselves in relationships. This is especially true if we are with the wrong person. We are forever worried and concerned that if we muck up, they will leave us. We become 'yes' people, or people pleasers. Perhaps we can relate this back to some abandonment issues, or perhaps not. It's different for everyone.

Of course, we are influenced by where we come from, how we grew up, who our role models were, including family, school friends, teachers, and many other people we looked up to or were exposed to. There are so many thoughts, beliefs, ideas, patterns of behaviour we unconsciously collect during our lives, particularly in our formative years. This may be why even siblings growing up in the same family can have totally different ideas or opinions as adults. We are all exposed to vastly differing external influences at pivotal points in our lives. The good news is that no matter how we arrived at today, we have the power to change today and our direction in the future. The key here is to make a choice. At the very beginning of the book, I posed the question of when NOW would be an ideal time for change. We use excuses and point fingers, and avoiding the present moment

## The Cracks Appear

by finding other reasons it's not the right time. NOW, is always the best time to start living and thriving! The cracks soon appear when we think about things differently. You can't un-think thinking differently, it changes everything!

We all have different ways of thinking. We often think we need to think the same as another to belong and thus lose our ability to think for ourselves. We can even forget that we should honour our own thoughts and feelings first. Saying that, we must also make sure we are open to learning new things, ways and solutions. How else do we continue to thrive and grow? Just because something held true five minutes, weeks or even years ago doesn't mean there isn't new knowledge and an opportunity to upgrade our brains. Far too often, people get stuck in their ways and unfortunately shut out any opportunity to grow and experience life in new and different ways. I find it so sad that so many are closed down to new experiences through fear and because this is the way it's always been, or "I'm too old to change!"

Fear is responsible for so much of what is happening inside us and in the world around us. Unless there is something real that is threatening us physically, fear is just False Expectations that Appear Real.

Fear triggers the imagination of the brain, and this can play havoc with what is actually real and what is not. It is almost comical when you think about it consciously. We worry continuously about things that aren't even real, they simply don't exist. This causes us to live in constant overdrive, or as it now known, survival mode. As a species, we were never meant or even built to operate in this state on a continuous level. Physiologically, this state is only meant for when we are being chased by a sharped toothed animal or some other external force. When you take a step back and look at the state of the world these days, it becomes quite apparent why it's happening. Everything has become so fast, busy and hurried, instant gratification is expected. From being impatient that a red light doesn't go green quickly enough to receiving your Uber fast meal just isn't fast enough. The simple pleasure of having 'gaps' in your day where you can just enjoy a few moments to yourself without checking your phone, like waiting for an appointment, being stuck in traffic, being held up for whatever reason. These are perfect opportunities to resist distractions and just stop and look around you. Sit on a park bench, take a breath and take it in. Allow yourself the luxury of a break.

## The Cracks Appear

Even when people go on holidays, they go somewhere to relax but they want to 'do' things they don't do in everyday life. People have forgotten how it is to just BE and not DO. It's a holiday, so just STOP! This inability to stop and then wonder why they get back from their holiday and then 'need a holiday' to get over their holiday.

It's no wonder why so many of us are in such poor health, both physically and mentally. There is no downtime, no gaps. If there is a spare moment, it's eyes down, glued to their phones or screens, scrolling. There are now generations emerging who do not know how to enjoy life. They are so caught up in everyone else's lives, they forget how to live their own. This seriously concerns me. If you miss the gaps, you're missing living. Here's a little exercise to do when you have gaps in your day. Consciously leave your phone in your pocket, watch people—notice how many are rushing, on their phones, distracted, how many are actually paying attention? I love looking at ants or insects. It brings you into the moment of right now. It's fascinating what you see when you look.

*When you surrender to what is and so become fully present, the past ceases to have any power. Presence is the key. The Now is the key.*

**Eckhart Tolle**

Anxiety levels and panic attacks seem to be skyrocketing out of control. Everyone seems to be glued to their phones or other technology. I see parents pushing or sitting with their child's pram, whilst on the phone. The child is looking at the parent, being and feeling ignored. The phone appears to be more important than them. This is the beginning of feeling unimportant or even unwanted. And so, the slippery slope begins. Young children are given a phone or tablet to keep the peace, while parents are 'too busy' to be present with their children when all the children really want and need is love and attention from their parents. I'm not saying take it all away, but it would be beneficial to have boundaries and balance so they can learn how to self-regulate (this applies to adults as well). Adults need to control their use of device time and teach their children how to do the same. There needs to be a balance between real time and screen time! What I hear from people today, both young and old is that the 'screen time' function is hardly used, and they haven't learnt to enjoy being present and spending time in nature as perhaps us humans once did. Nature and being in it is vital to our health and wellbeing as human beings. We were not meant for sitting inside, sedentary and glued to screens. There are so many digital games and applications creating incredible levels of sensory overload and we need to

## The Cracks Appear

know how to simply turn it off and relax our senses and find longer gaps for our nervous system to simply have a break.

It's no wonder divorce rates are high. How many of us go to bed and scroll aimlessly before turning the lights out? How many kids take their devices to bed with them, like a security blanket? How many of us meditate, download, and get rid of the day's stresses so we can sleep peacefully? Babies are now often born into a state of immediate stress and it's showing up more and more. If parents are stressed, even while the baby is in the womb, the baby may likely be affected well before they even take their first breath. We have moved so far away from the sanctity and role of the 'mother' and the nurturing required from the get-go. We have generations of patriarchy and power being stripped from the woman, it's become confusing, and as women, we are finding out quickly that we are not superhuman. We have been led to believe that we can be 'super-mums'. The cracks in this fabric are taking their toll and women feel like failures when they realise they simply cannot sustain being a 'super-mum' over a long period. In addition, they have forgotten how to feel as a mother. It's too hard, and it's too taxing. You can't expect a woman to know how it's going to feel or what to expect going into motherhood, and perhaps the only person who can nurture and install this knowing is your own mother. I know that's where I learnt that from. I'd be interested if you, as a woman, had the same experience. I remember hearing a quote on fathers and parenting, it goes something like this: the best thing a father can do for his children is to love their mother. It is self-explanatory.

The vortex of negative mind chatter is exacerbated while pregnant. Couple this with hormones and today's expectations and you've got yourself and incredibly stressful time. Being a busy, successful working woman is seen to be more the norm now, and in addition to generally being the cook, cleaner, planner, accountant and everyone's 'dogsbody'. It's no wonder we're stressed and suffer postnatal depression and anxiety! Fortunately, many men have and are stepping up and are taking on more 'chores' in this space now. They are more involved with children than they were fifty years ago. Saying that, many men are confused as to what their role is these days, as many had very little guidance from their own absent fathers.

So, what can we do about this? What is the solution? First, this question is loaded with significant variables such as where you're from, family history, emotional

## The Cracks Appear

presence and intelligence, religious beliefs and many more. Everyone has a different story, and the fact is we all take on information differently based on our own perception of our inner world. What this means in simple terms is, two people can have exactly the same experience but attach two very different meanings to it. For example, if two people are asked to go on a rollercoaster ride, the immediate response is highly likely to be two opposing views. One will be super excited, whilst the other is about to melt down and have a panic attack without even going anywhere near the ride. It is all about the 'meaning' we or our minds rather, attach to a situation. If we can control the meaning of a situation, we control our results and how we feel.

It is this simple, yet so complex. The key here is to understand that we are a product of our external world, but the 'actual' key here is that we are in control of how we respond to the external world. How we think and process the external information coming in is what creates our experience. In a nutshell, it's the old saying by Henry Ford, "Whether you think can, or think you can't, you are right." I grew up with my dad telling me, "You can." So, for me, that has always been with me. I have told myself a million times, I can do this, and when I have applied it, it has guided me well. Unfortunately, so many have not had this embedded mantra and find life is full of roadblocks, failures, and blame anyone and everything for the situation they find themselves in. It can be tough to be positive or forward thinking if you've never been taught how.

As we humans have evolved, we have gone from living simply to simply living. During the last fifty years, the technological and scientific advances have occurred at a crazy and exponential rate. Going from computers only being available to governments and their agencies, to having access to a supercomputer in your pocket in the shape of your mobile phone. If you grew up in an era where the only way you could walk and talk on a phone was to buy a curly extension cord and plug it in to the actual base of the telephone attached to the wall. Even then you were lucky if you could move more than a few metres. The plastic (petroleum) revolution had arrived and everything that once rusted or decomposed, was replaced with plastic that lasts hundreds and hundreds of years, like buckets. Unfortunately, when the handle on the bucket breaks, they become useless and get thrown away without even thinking twice, out of sight and out of mind.

## The Cracks Appear

When something is deemed broken, it's thrown away. This is why it's so important to choose wisely with everything we acquire, whether it's during our grocery shop or even our partners. According to a 2023 Australian Institute of Family Studies report, 44% of marriages end in divorce. I'm not sure about you, but I think that's high. This issue is once again rife with variables. So many external things influence a successful marriage. From choosing a partner just because they 'look' good and striving to have the most spectacular wedding event in human history, to the ever present and rising epidemic of domestic violence (including the increasing number of associated deaths) and straight-out abuse.

Abuse comes in many shapes and sizes. You have the overt physical violence to the covert passive aggressive type that controls in underhanded ways, and even many combinations of both. It's not a simple thing to manage and often we don't even see the abuse is occurring until something significant happens or until you're out of the relationship and can look back. Only then, the patterns of control become blindingly obvious. Whether through money, children, lies, or deceit, it is abuse, and it is unacceptable. Emotional or psychological abuse is deemed to be just as devastating and sometimes worse than physical violence. Either way, there are no excuses.

> *NOTE: If you, or someone you know, are in this type of situation, get in touch with the Domestic Violence Service or Woman's Rescue in your area for guidance and help.*

There are so many things during our life that can, in both big and small ways, influence how we get to where we are today. I know it's cliche, but time really does fly by quickly. Especially when you are in a 'dream state' and just going through the motions of life. You may be becoming more conscious and aware of your surroundings and questioning yourself about what is happening around you and around the world. There seems to be more and more people waking up and thinking, *is this it?* It can be a subtle nudge or a massive jolt! However, it shows up for you, make sure you take notice of what it feels like. Are there any messages or warnings? For me, it's been a combination of messages and sometimes very subtle intuitive feelings to my life being physically threatened by someone I loved. The biggest downfall or issue here is when we totally ignore these messages and make excuses for others, blame ourselves or just plain 'suck it up' because somehow we tell ourselves we deserve to be mistreated.

## The Cracks Appear

One thing you must know, and that is that it's never too late! As long as you are breathing and know that something has to change, it is never too late to change your circumstances. The sad thing is that people accept living in misery and tell themselves that *this is the bed I've made, so I have to lie in it.* WRONG! This is never the case. The only thing wrong is what we tell ourselves. Whether we continue to lie to ourselves that everything FINE (F'd up, Insecure, Neurotic and Emotional) or whether we are simply too fearful to make the decision to change our situation. It falls in the too hard basket for so many and that is where they end up on their deathbed with a long list of regrets.

In Bronnie Ware's book, *Top Five Regrets of the Dying (2011)*, she lists the most common regrets as:

1. I wish I'd had the courage to live a life true to myself, not the life others expected of me.
2. I wish I hadn't worked so hard.
3. I wish I'd had the courage to express my feelings.
4. I wish I had stayed in touch with my friends.
5. I wish that I had let myself be happier.

Almost everyone has some regrets. It is interesting to note the number one reason is not living a life true to oneself. This speaks volumes, particularly when you are in a situation where you know deep down it is not for you, you are staying for someone or something else. Honesty is always the best policy. Find the courage to speak up and foremost, be honest with yourself.

It is just as important to know that sometimes it is imperative to extract yourself from toxic relationships, particularly violent and psychologically abusive ones. Especially where the safety of yourself and your children is at risk.

Make sure that when you are taking steps towards significant changes in your life that you do not walk over loved ones. Be open and honest about where you are at and why it is important to you to make these changes. For example, I have had clients who have gone on a journey of personal growth and, for health reasons, change their eating and exercise habits. While their partner was initially on board and supportive, as soon as the changes started becoming visible and significant, they sabotage, mock and disempower the person making the changes. This is quite a common response from partners who are not wanting to change or grow themselves. They feel like they're trailing behind and consciously or unconsciously drag their partner back to their own

## The Cracks Appear

level. Often, this manipulation works and leaves the person trying to make positive change back at square one. Something to look out for if you are making the decision to improve your own health and wellbeing through personal development and growth.

Ideally, make these decisions to change as a couple so that you support and grow together. Don't ignore the signs. Attempt to repair and rejuvenate the love you once had, and if that doesn't bear fruit, be consciously kind to each other and loved ones around you.

It is important to acknowledge that as we grow older and have been with the same person for a long time, it takes effort to keep your relationship alive and thriving. There are constant life challenges coming at us and if your communication and priority to each other is waning, you can become easily disconnected, distant, disenchanted, and things become disjointed and difficult. To enable positive change, someone must open the lines of honest communication without judgment and blame. This comes easily to some, but many do not know where to begin or even engage. We need to ask ourselves, *how have I contributed to the current situation, what do I need to own?* Even then, for some, it can be the beginning of the end of their relationship, but that can also be amicable and comes with new beginnings for both parties. Whatever happens, there are always new ways to see things and options to live a fabulous life. Infidelity is a tricky one, but inexcusable, and the offending party needs to own it and be honest about it as the truth always comes out at some point. Shit happens and people must take responsibility for their actions and not shift the blame from themselves just because it's too hard.

So how can we avoid the end-of-life regrets? The first thing to do is to take action. No matter how small, every journey begins with a first step. Doing one thing every day that differs from your normal routine will help shift your direction. Meditation is one of those small steps that has a big impact. If you start with a good morning and evening meditation every day, you will notice a difference in how you are feeling, both emotionally and mentally, within a short space of time. The key is consistency and doing it daily is ideal, though don't stress if you miss a day. If you stick with it, meditation will have a huge impact on general wellbeing. Another example is writing down three things you are grateful for twice a day. Again, morning and evening are good times for this. Though you can choose when is best for you, especially if you're a shift worker or have a busy routine already,

## The Cracks Appear

make the time available for you. It's great to have a special notebook and pen that looks and feels nice for writing your thoughts down. It makes it more tactile and inspiring. Don't wait, do it today.

Do things that inspire you. If you hate your job and can't change this in the short term, find new ways/thoughts that can make your day brighter. For example, if you work with someone that gets on your nerves, you can be curious as to why you are choosing to let them get under your skin. Ask yourself why am I triggered? Know that when someone else triggers you, it is a reflection of you, and it may be there is something about yourself that you need to look at and change. It could be a small, simple thing or it could be more complex that you may need some guidance with. Triggers are interesting. It is important to note that it is not the trigger itself that creates this issue, it is the meaning we attach to a trigger event that will make you come unstuck. Practice catching your thoughts next time you are triggered, identfy and change the meaning you attach to the trigger. You will feel very different if you attach a positive meaning. It's a fun game I like to play.

Surround yourself with more like minded people. If you change your inner world, i.e. your thoughts and emotions, it creates a ripple effect on your outer world. Often, you'll find negative people around will try to suck you back into the vortex and managing this can be challenging. There are gentle ways to extract yourself from negative people, particularly family members. The old saying, "you can choose your friends, but you can't choose your family," is absolute bollocks. Time and time again, my clients have shown me this: sometimes a clear shut down is necessary and other times it is all about perspective. How you see and act in a relationship is up to you, and you can choose to acknowledge a person for who they are, accept it, but not allow it to enter your inner world and peace. It takes practice, but it works and soon becomes second nature.

> *Don't take anything personally. Nothing others do is because of you. What others say and do is a projection of their own reality, their own dream. When you are immune to the opinions and actions of others, you won't be the victim of needless suffering.*
>
> **Don Miguel Ruiz**

## The Cracks Appear

Be a duck! It sounds strange, but I'm sure you've heard of the saying, "like water off a duck's back." If not, you may have noticed how duck feathers protect the duck's skin from water from penetrating through when diving. They also assist the duck with buoyancy. Keeping your own mind dry and buoyant is imperative when you are on your journey of growth. When you allow words and actions of others to penetrate your inner world, you give away your power and become the victim of what others say and do. We are only responsible for ourselves and what we think, feel, and do. We have no business in anyone else's business. What they say, feel and do has nothing to do with us and it's time that everyone stops thinking that other people's opinions matter. Yes, they matter to them and what we think matters to us. We cannot expect other people to think the same way we do. We can chat and often agree on things and try to show different angles to look at things, but we cannot order people to agree with us. Forcing our thoughts and opinions on others, or vice versa, only creates a divide and leaves both parties feeling like shit.

To manage this, take a virtual step back from the negative energy of a person or situation. BE A DUCK and know that it's not about you! Humans have a terrible habit of projecting their insecurities, shame, and emotions outwardly because it is hard to look at themselves. I have done this many times over the years and it takes awareness to stop negative projection. After all, we are only human and there is no such thing as a perfect person. The important thing is to be honest with yourself, take responsibility for your stuff and own it. It's a tough one, but very doable.

Choose happiness. Yes, it's a choice and we are only responsible for our own happiness. No-one else's. Of course, if you are a parent of small children, or even grown children, we are responsible for guiding them along the way to ensure they know how to choose happiness. It's sounds simple, but as my best friend said to me years ago, "it takes a lot more courage to be happy than it does to be miserable." To this day, it still echoes in my mind and is still a great reminder it's up to me to choose happiness, or to choose to wallow in my own misery. A smile can instantly turn negative emotions into positive emotions. Try it now. Now, turn your smile around and create a frown. Notice the difference? If you catch yourself feeling down, just put a smile on face, even if it is fake to start with—if you keep the smile on your dial, you will start to feel it. It can change the whole trajectory and has the potential to turn your whole day around!

## The Cracks Appear

This is an effective way to change your day, but more importantly, your inner voice is even more important. The way we talk to ourselves in our mind plays a huge role in how we think, feel, and act.

Another effective way of changing your day is being kinder to yourself and to talking to yourself as a five-year-old. You'll soon discover how much damage you can do to your inner self and happiness when you consciously listen to your own bullshit and negativity. Treat yourself with the love, kindness, and respect you deserve. That we all deserve. Choose self-love and care and think of your much older future self and what they would say to your present self. How would you guide yourself forward? Would you tell them to stay in the vortex of negativity or suggest they do some inner work, so they can get on and live life to the max from here on? Would you suggest perhaps revisiting a lifelong dream on your bucket list or dare I say it, start ticking off the *old one day I'll or one day I'd love to… lists?* I can guarantee your older self would tell you to pull that proverbial finger out and get on it! Start ticking off those dreams and create your new reality.

Q: What is currently stopping you from living your best life? What is one thing you can you do from today that can shift this (even if it is only a small thing)?

Date: _____

_____
_____
_____
_____
_____

## CHAPTER 9

# Golden Repair

*When you realise everyone is a projection of how they feel internally, you take a whole lot less to heart.*

**Unknown**

You may recognise or identify with some things mentioned in previous chapters. No matter what has happened in the past, know you can't change it, but there are so many ways you can glue the pieces back together and make it whole again. It will look and feel a little different, but it is worth the effort it takes to put the pieces together and make it stronger than ever before. It may seem impossible at the start, that's why it is so important to take it one piece at a time. The result will surprise and delight you.

There are no shortcuts here and it certainly can be hard but in the main you will find if you follow the steps and do the work your life will be better than ever. Make no mistake, life will continue to throw you curve balls. The important thing is to get the foundations deeply and firmly solid so you can weather any storm or vortex that presents itself. If you do this, you will know exactly how to respond and not fall back into 'react' mode and repeat old patterns. This can be scary, and you will need to retreat temporarily, stabilise and re-check yourself.

First things first, before you step out and into something new, especially growth and change, you need to be 100% ready and make a conscious decision about what you are embarking on and know what result you are wanting. It will take time (perhaps not as long as you think though), work, investment and effort. If you choose to go ahead, the best news is that you will notice a positive change almost immediately.

## Golden Repair

1. Clarity: what is the result do you want to achieve? Be clear before you start. If you don't know then seek guidance—get a free consultation as your first point of reference.
2. Research: find tools or modalities of healing/growth that resonate with you. If it feels right and fits what you want to achieve, look into it further.
3. Choose: a guide (coach, mentor, therapist) to assist your transformation. Feel if there is 'trust' there, no pushing or selling and they are genuine. You need to resonate with your guide for best results.
4. Get ready and press GO!

If you choose to go it alone, via research on the internet, for example, look for tools that will help with changing the way you think and bring calm to your inner world. for example, meditation—find a voice or sounds that resonate and soothe you. This is so important and is such a personal choice. The likelihood of consistency in mediation rests on you finding the right style and frequency for you. If you haven't meditated before, guided meditations are a great place to start. It's easy to find via google, You tube, Spotify, Apple Music etc. There are meditations for stress, sleep, clarity, calm, success, and so much more. The important thing is to find those that resonate with you and start your daily practice. Guided meditations, like Yoga Nidra, are great for alleviating a busy or 'monkey mind'. Don't get caught up thinking you need to have a blank mind—it takes a bit of practice to get there and the reality is we are not monks, and we have lots going on in our lives. Accept that however the meditation is for you on any particular day, will be different and will be right for you on that day. Some days it can be really challenging but persevere and it will get easier with time.

Books are also a fabulous resource, especially now with audio books. It makes it easier to listen and digest more content if you don't have/make time to sit down and read. Some of my personal favourites include Louise Hay's *You Can Heal Your Life*, *The Power of Now* (2004) by Eckhart Tolle, *The Wisdom of Florence Scovel Shinn* (1989), *Breaking the Habit of Being Yourself* (2012) by Joe Dispenza, *Meditation Pure and Simple* by Ian Gawler (1996), *The Portal* (book – 2019 and movie) by Tom Cronin and Jacqui Fifer, *Think Like a Monk by Jay Shetty (2020)*, and too many more to list here. Once again, look for those that resonate with you. A recommended further reading list is attached at the end of this book as a starting point. It is amazing how many books you can 'read' now with audio book 'apps'. Personally, I still prefer to hold and physically read books. I feel there is more connection with the author that way, but again each to their own, as long as you do it is what matters here.

Finding the right person to work with can be a daunting task. Word of mouth and referrals are often a great place to start. Ask close friends or trusted colleagues if they know of anyone in your area. Your doctor can also be a good resource. The important thing here is finding a person with whom you feel comfortable with and feel a sense of trust from the minute you first meet or chat online. It is easy to get caught up in all types of healing modalities such as breathwork, hypnosis, Cognitive Behaviour Therapy, traditional therapies, and the like, so it's important to go with what makes the most sense and feels right for you. Provided you are doing the work and recommended tasks, if something is not working or feels off (after a reasonable period of time), I recommend reviewing your relationship from an unbiased point of view. If you are certain it's not self-sabotage or limiting beliefs, then it may be time to move on to someone else who will fit you better. We are all so different and need to connect with our inner self in the way that makes the most sense to you. For me, that is having a great mentor, daily meditation, yoga and hypnosis.

I wish I had given myself permission and strength to stand in my power and not wait to make the changes. I was caught up in doing the right thing, even though it felt so wrong inside. I listened to what other people were saying, instead of my own inner voice.

I wish I'd listened to my intuition. Thought from a higher place, seen a bigger picture of the situation. The the words and intentions were there, but the actions did not align with the promises. Taking a step back is imperative when something feels wrong or inconsistent. Only then can we see what it is truly happening. Noting behaviours, including the way someone judges others, dishonours and demeans you and others, especially in front of loved ones. This is incredibly hurtful and harmful behaviour and should be called out for what it is and that is passive aggressive belittling. It is cowardly and has no place in a relationship.

I wish I had the foresight to see beyond the facades and acknowledge the underhanded remarks and comments and bowed out earlier. But love can create extreme blindness, and you only see want you want to see and hope that somehow things will change or at least be okay. These lessons are hard for those of us who believe in love and see the goodness and potential in people beyond face value. You hope that one day they will wake up and see it for themselves, but in my experience, it's a waste of time. *What you tolerate, you validate.* If you allow people to treat you poorly and accept it, that is what you are inviting and what you will get. I certainly wish I knew this a very long time ago. I always thought seeing the good in people was the important thing. Turns out seeing the good in yourself is the most important thing.

*Respect the past and create the future.*

On that note, as you collect your scars along the way and you may have a few or you may have a truck load, there are many ways to move beyond your scars and live a beautiful and fulfilling life. Acknowledging and honouring your scars is a huge part of moving forward, not reliving them over and over, but just knowing that they happened, and it takes time and effort to repair the pieces of your heart and put the pieces back together. That's why I love the cover of this book, it traces the cracks, the breaks, the heartache we go through, but also shows the incredible beauty that ensues by putting it all back together.

One of the best parts of starting fresh, is to dig up some old dreams and live life to the fullest every second of every day. There are so many cliches written on this and each one is true, especially the one about the fact that being present is our *present*. There are no guarantees for tomorrow, no taking back yesterday only what you have right now and what you do with each minute infront of you. Don't wait for the 'perfect time' or 'I'll do it when…' It doesn't exist. You have to make things happen and bring your dreams to life. No one else can or will do this for you. It's your life, make the decision and just do it.

Q: How often do you consciously learn new things? What has been your biggest 'aha' moment in this Chapter?

Date: _____

_____
_____
_____
_____
_____

## CHAPTER 10

# I am Me; I Am Love

*Your visions will become clear only when you can look into your own heart. Who looks outside, dreams; who looks inside, awakes.*

**Carl Jung**

So now it's time to wake up, time to tune in and face the music. Time to ask some hard questions and give yourself the truth and be totally honest. There is a bit of a road ahead to navigate and it will be different for everyone. Tell no lies, then you don't have to remember anything! No matter what, honesty is always best, especially when it comes to yourself. You cannot heal unless you are honest and dig deep and know that we are all mere humans doing the best we can with the information we have on hand.

If you can see beyond your ego and look at this beautiful planet we live on as a small part of the great universe, it gives us perspective of how small we are but also how important we are as part of a finely tuned global ecosystem. It must be recognised that as a species we have fallen way short of doing our part within this finite system. We need to come back to this perspective and look at how we fit in with the rest of the millions of species on the planet and what we can all do to behave in a more symbiotic way so that some restoration can begin.

To gain peace on the planet, we must first gain peace within. We must have new ways and new systems globally. Nature can and will teach us all we need to know how to go about this and the wonderful Sir David Attenborough gives us so much insight to where to start as a species. But first, we need to heal ourselves and reconnect at a deep level. Technology has created overwhelm by inundating us with millions of bits of information at an alarming pace. We simply cannot take it all in. It is creating a connection of world-wide cultures that we have never seen before and with this comes infinite real potential for global change.

Unfortunately, at present it is creating grief and disharmony on so many levels we are forgetting how to behave and process the simplest of things. It's no wonder ADHD and neuro diverse ailments have become the modern epidemic. People of all ages are unable to cope with everyday life now. Which is why we must start by regaining our balance as individuals, as couples, as communities, as cities and countries around the world. We need to take a global approach whilst acting locally for the greater good.

So how do we do this? Well, it's the scars we carry and what we can learn from our healing journeys that hold the key. Which is why we start from scratch, as outlined in the previous chapter. It needs to be a simple process even though it's a challenging journey once we get to the point of perspective and understanding that we are at breaking point as a species and we need to think collectively, feel and act from our hearts instead of our heads. Heart-based action will outweigh any obstacle, and that is why when we are making any decision, large or small, we must start there. We must break our old patterns and cycles. They are outdated and we need to find and create new solutions. Watch children from anywhere in the world. What do they do? They love to play, run, laugh with anyone else in the vicinity. It's the purity of this that needs to be our foundation.

Music is another foundation of joy and love. I see it on the faces of children and adults learning to play instruments or going to concerts. Again, it has a purity and is essential in healing and connection. Next time you watch a concert with a stadium full of people all singing in unison, look at their smiles, the pure joy. It's magical.

Remember, we are all in this together and we are all part of the 'human condition' (it is recommended to research this topic for perspective). Start small, like just practicing your self-talk, self-love, and connect to your heart space. Write down three things you are grateful for everyday to remind yourself that you have a choice to see the good things in your life and around you. Remember, it all starts with you and how you shape your thoughts and what you do to honour your inner peace. I'll say it again: meditation is like an injection of mind and soul juice that flows through the whole body. Practice at least twice per day and remember, everyone's meditation can be different. Some days are harder to sit still, and others just seems to flow better. As my teacher, friend and mentor, Tom Cronin says, "It doesn't matter how deep you go. Even shallow meditations will have a significant impact on you. It will kick off a new path towards love and peace."

Another simple thing you can do is write your 'non-negotiables' and introduce one new thing that you can do daily honour yourself and feel good. Non-negotiables are those things YOU love to do just for you, things that put a smile on your face. They are all about de-exciting your nervous system, slowing things down for even just a few minutes to reset and make you feel good. Easy examples are to go for a walk and while you're on that walk, see everything around with the eyes of your five-year-old self. If you can't go for a walk, stop and look out your window and see the wonders all around you. Notice the little things like lady bugs, trees with interesting leaves or branches, how green the grass is, those tiny blades of grass growing impossibly through concrete and so on. I'm sure you get what I'm saying, be aware of the good things and focus on them. Where thoughts go, energy flows, think good thoughts.

Doing your non-negotiables list with your partner is a great exercise for couples to encourage re-connection once again. Focus on what you both love together and start introducing these on a daily, weekly, even monthly must-do's to strengthen your communication. This is time for the two of you, not time for house stuff. This is heart stuff. Keep it simple, speak and breathe through your hearts. Honour yourselves together and feel what it is to have this person in your life and make time and space amid the busy-ness.

We must realise that while we are in good health, mobile and sharp in our brain, which is a muscle we must exercise to stay sharp (Limitless by Jim Kwik, 2020). Honour your dreams or at least some of them. As Bronnie Ware wrote, "It is very important to try and honour at least some of your dreams along the way, from the moment that you lose your health, it is too late. Health brings a freedom very few realise, until they no longer have it" (2019). Lowering your cortisol and adrenalin levels will go a long way to looking after your health. We are living in a state of fast times and are in constant fight or flight mode. This is not good! It is time slow down!

# I am Me; I Am Love

Q: Be brutally honest here, what are you doing (or thinking) that is keeping you stuck? What lie are you telling yourself that may serve as your excuse/reason for not moving forward and living your best life?

Date: _____

_____

_____

_____

_____

_____

## CHAPTER 11

# Living Life Now

*Presence is needed to become aware of the beauty, the majesty, the sacredness of nature.*
**Eckhart Tolle**

The importance of presence in our lives can be the difference between merely existing within our own self-imposed boundaries and living a truly free and fulfilling life. Many wealthy and successful people are incredibly depressed and lack meaning and happiness because their lives have become so complex and consumed with a fear of losing everything they have. Indeed, many have lost everything many times over as a result of often unconsciously focussing on the energy of fear and lack. Thankfully, these days many more astute and aware wealthy people are supporting change and new solutions for the planet and its people. These people have learned to connect their heart with their brain and think first, feel into their heart and act accordingly.

Think, feel, do!

Aligned with this process, are your personal values, also known as your personal compass. Without your compass, your decision making becomes erratic and directionless. Like a ship's captain in a fog without a clue on how or where to steer the ship. This is why we end up marooned or shipwrecked in our own life. A huge part of our journey back to ourselves is getting clear on our values and what is important to us, not only materially, but more importantly, spiritually and physically. This is also where our intuition kicks in. Several of my clients have had a look of *wow, I've never thought of that*. But this is where the clarity comes in and the compass bearings are divulged. It gives a surety about who we are and what we can do for ourselves and how we can contribute to make this planet better than it was when we arrived. It's a feeling of freedom and direction at the same time.

I chose not to listen to my inner self/compass and intuition, which led my actions to become incongruent with my values and what I stand for. Because of this misalignment, it created dis-ease internally, and I became ill at various points. I was so deep in the pit, and it was getting deeper by the day. I used band-aids and notional bandages to cover, deflect and slowly lost all sense of self and hope. There was no way forward or out of the pit. I did not realise I had all the tools I needed inside all along. I just had to find them. I soon realised that the universe knows, and if you let it in, it has totally got your back. It will guide and lead you to the right doors. As soon as I changed my situation, good things and people started coming into my life to guide me on my way. I had faith in life again and believed from my core that there was way, a path, one foot in front of the other and before I knew it, I felt a change inside and was back on track.

I didn't have all the knowledge and tools I have today, which is why I want to share them with you in this book and through my coaching and, at the very least, do my best to make a difference both locally and globally. To encourage and show there is a way and inspire you to make a start on your own journey. We are all in different places in our lives and have different paths to tread.

Don't think, just start! There will be many obstacles and challenges, but there's always a way forward if you come back to your heart, gut and mind in that order. It's where love resides, and it will always ground you if you take a few moments to breathe deeply and connect. When you get hit with something, breathe in and out of your heart first. It will guide and settle you every time. I fully understand that when you are in the thick of 'shitsville', it is difficult to stop and do this, but we must. Listen to a beautiful piece of music or a favourite song. Take your shoes off and ground yourself to the earth beneath you, meditate. Do whatever works to bring you back to calm.

The things that I considered and planned for to extract myself safely when I was 'stuck' in a toxic relationship include:

- Deciding to leave a relationship when you finally acknowledge there's nothing left that you could do to save it.
- Acknowledge change can be hard and extremely testing of your whole being. You

need to build courage and strength, like training for an event or competition.
- Protect yourself and your children from narcissistic/abusive behaviour—connect with experts or agencies who are there to help, e.g. Women's Refuge, Lifeline, and other organisations, to assist you exit safely.
- Once you have made the choice to leave, plan what to take with you like special items that cannot be replaced etc. Speak only to people you can trust fully as this is a very delicate process and you don't want to raise suspicions putting yourself (and children) in more danger. Again, get help from the appropriate agencies to ensure safety.
- Ensure children are safe, psychologically, and physically.
- What logistics need to be identified and arranged as much as possible prior to leaving?
- A recommended lawyer or firm waiting in the wings can also be good for support and advice. However, if you can avoid this after the initial help, then do. It can be a very expensive, drawn-out exercise.
- Start building your self-esteem with a counsellor in person and/or online courses to help gain clarity, build courage and strength.

This is vital. Please note this takes a little time, as we have generally been living in survival mode for a long time and logic may also be blurred.
- If you are fortunate enough to be with someone who is not too extreme in their controlling behaviour, a mutual uncoupling is best for everyone.
- Remember to be kind to yourself and do not compare yourself to anyone else's experience. It's different for everyone.
- It may seem it's easier to stay, as you know what you're getting already, but it is worth fighting for your (and your children's) freedom.
- Fear of being left with nothing is always at the front of mind, but the bottom line is: if you (and kids) get out safely, then that's the biggest and most important reason in the world. Being prepared and knowing what freedom is worth helps to alleviate this thought pattern.

There is no sugar coating it. Going through this kind of journey is massive. It takes its toll. Would I change anything? Yes, there are a few things I would change or do differently, but I know everything I went through was absolutely worth it. I have grown on so many levels and I am still on my ongoing journey to be the best person I can be. I know now how important it is for me to help others for the greater good in any way I can. This includes my own self health and wellbeing and being the best I can be as a mum, in my work, and as a citizen on this beautiful planet.

It is impossible for anyone to maintain this level of commitment to a high level all the time, and I too need to continue to be present and watch my thoughts and behaviour patterns. It's so easy to slip. Always remember, NO ONE AND NOTHING IS PERFECT. I just remind myself consistently to be as conscious of my thoughts, feeling and actions. And I absolutely must grab myself by the scruff of the neck and give myself an 'atti-tunement'—also known as an 'attitude adjustment' every once in a while! 'Atti-tunement' is a new phrase coined by my bestie, I loved it so much, I had to include it in this book.

My scars are and will always be present, and small things still trigger old wounds. But I am learning every day to attach new meanings to them and that they are only vague memories. Little veins of gold that continue to mend and restore my heart as I learn and grow every day. I am still healing and under no illusion that I won't need more gold to fill in new cracks in the future. All I know is that I am not broken, just a little mis-aligned some days. I think people use the term 'broken' too much. It becomes difficult to then let the word and thought go and we get stuck in the healing vortex as a result. We can get stuck on a perpetual quest to find something external to heal us. I like to use the golden repair metaphor instead, as it gives hope and creates a new, stronger perception of our hearts and what we have been through. The immense strength and love the scars I carry within me give me is incredible and I feel so powerful in my integrity and purpose. It amazes me every day. I love looking at my scars in this way. I give them acknowledgement, but not the power to define who I truly am. This is my wish for you too.

*Joy does not simply happen to us. We have to choose joy and keep choosing it every day.*

**Henri Nouwen**

Q: What can you THINK, FEEL and DO now to change your whole perspective on how you are currently living? Again, you need to be brutally honest with yourself and think deeply about how you want to see yourself and your life in the next 1 – 3 years.

Date: _____

_____

_____

_____

_____

_____

# CHAPTER 12

# Choose Now

*You must unload, to unfold.*

Congratulations! You've made it this far! I trust you have found the starting point for your own journey. Now grab on to something tightly and get ready to soar into your future.

Have you ever asked yourself sometimes, *haven't I been through enough* or *here we go again, why does this always happen to me?* Well, no more. It's now time to kick those old patterns and receive the messages you need to hear with open ears and an open heart. It's time to move forward. It's time to get that needle out of the scratch in the old record and maybe even start playing a new record! Whatever and however you choose to play, just play it loud and proud, okay!!

The aim of this book is to highlight how we get caught and lost in our stories, whether it be diminished self-esteem through the fear of violence and abuse or if you've just lost your way through internal pain. Know that now is always the best time to bring clarity and happiness back into your life. One choice, one day at a time and total commitment to be honest with yourself and do the work is all you need. A golden quote from Keith Urban: "it is not your fault, but it is your responsibility and it's okay to ask for help."

We must be real about who we are and the role we play in our own suffering. It is perfectly summed up by Billy Chapata, who on X wrote, "Being honest about the role you played in your own suffering opens up paths back to yourself. Accountability with yourself opens up new doorways to your healing," (Billy Chapata, 2022). This is a most bitter pill to swallow, and it is your choice if you want to continue to stay in victim mode.

Spirituality is pivotal in the process; this does not mean becoming religious (unless it's aligned in a healthy way with your journey). It is part of re-connecting with your inner self, your own higher spirit, your inner God. This can be a daunting path as it may challenge conventional religious beliefs. However, just know that peace, love, and happiness come from within, not from with-out. You and only you are responsible for it. Meditation is the path to reconnecting with yourself, and it is the most beautiful way back to yourself. Finding you again is the path to freedom and becoming whole again and being hopeful for what's coming. If we all feel this way globally, imagine what a beautiful world we will live in. This is my mission.

The most valuable tool I give to my clients is validation and allow them to be heard with zero judgement and, if they are ready and willing, I guide them gently on their path to peace. No one is perfect. In fact, there is NO perfect. There is only the pursuit and journey of self-awareness and love. Once we acknowledge that we have done and still do things as a consequence of our personal story and journey so far, then we are able to own our choices and decisions. We choose who and what we are. We are responsible for our own future, no one or nothing else. Before you even start the journey, the most important thing is to DECIDE that you are willing to do whatever it takes to grow, change what you need to and move forward in a more positive way. To good news is, that if we do the work, we can see progress and feel better quickly. Then it's all about consistent positive actions (choices) and acknowledging that there will be challenges, it's part of human life. However, as we grow, our ability to respond to them becomes less and less challenging and life becomes more stable with less extremes. You can think of it like waves on the ocean, they undulate nicely then a storm hits. When we learn to consciously ride the waves, seek safety and solitude, and help, we can prepared for anything.

How to get on the right track? The first step I took was to fully commit to my meditation practice. After years of trial, error and a lot of work, I learned to follow the following three steps each time I got knocked down by external forces and my own choices:

**Step 1.**

Meditation is not as difficult as you think. Many believe you have to stop and empty your mind.

## Choose Now

Particularly when you are new to meditation it is about sitting comfortably in stillness, let the thoughts flow and when you become aware of them, release them. It takes consistent practice and in time you will find that they will become less 'busy' and the mind chatter will subside. It is peaceful, grounding and great for reconnecting with ourselves. Two twenty minute meditations per day will change your life. To help give you a start, refer to the QR Codes at the end of this book that link to two meditations.

Your Morning Meditation and Your Evening Meditation. This will give you a kick start to your journey, at the very least! It is simple and, if used every day, very effective. All you need to do is listen first thing in the morning to set up your day and last thing at night before you go to sleep. These two meditations complement each other to release the day's stresses so you can have a peaceful sleep. Letting go of all the 'stuff' in your day allows your mind and body to renew, restore and reset each night and helps move you out of the vortex into a place of clarity and peace. When you wake up in the morning, whilst still in a semi-sleep state, the morning meditation reminds your brain to prepare for the day and gives you an anchor to deal with any difficult situations during the day. It is a circular process. Like a clock, it gives your mind and body time to release and reset at the beginning and end of each day. The more consistent you are with these two meditations, the more you will find that things become easier to manage and the future looks brighter each day. And if you don't like them, or the sound of my voice, look for some similar meditations. There are many free meditations out there and we all have individual tastes. The sound of a voice should not grate on you, it should calm you.

**Step 2.**

The next task to introduce is daily gratitude. It is as simple as being grateful for the little things, like waking up to a brand new day full of possibilities or watching birds fly against a blue sky. The key is to start remembering that there is always something to be grateful for, no matter how small. Normally, I would introduce this after the first full week of meditating. This step goes hand in hand with Step one. Write about three, or more, things you are grateful for each morning after your meditation. This will remind you and your brain of the good things that are around you. Do this both morning and evening for an extra boost. It is important not to get overwhelmed by doing too much too soon, but establishing a good daily self-care and self-love routine goes a long way to balance and support your nervous system and your mental health.

**Step 3.**

Introduce a daily (or, as a start, every other day) exercise routine. Walking is the easiest and healthiest way to do this. If you can't do this, find a good stretch/yoga class online (e.g. YouTube) and start there. Even if you begin with 10-15 minutes per day, it compounds over time. This is not a sprint; this is a long-term change to sync your mind and body. You need to do both inner work and outer work to create new neural pathways, patterns of thinking and patterns of behaviour.

The three steps above will begin the powerful process of change and start your journey back to *you*.

Remember:

1. Clarity is the secret sauce to creating change in your life.

2. Courage is built with conviction and time.
3. Continuity and consistency (good or bad) will create the future you choose.

The 'Three C's Program'* is the name of my program for positive change. It is a proven recipe and if followed and practiced daily, you will find the right path for you and achieve success. The program is based on years of trial and error and is what I found works best and is a guide to getting you back on and staying on track!

The following is a brief description of the pathway to living in sync with your goals and dreams:

**CLARITY:**
Having clarity about who we are is essential for all of us to enjoy our lives. As we meander through life, we often lose our sense of self in terms of what we do for work, the partners we choose, our relationships, our family history and so on. The busyness of life in general also does not encourage us to go within and stay in touch with ourselves. The first phase is all about you and where you are currently and where you want to go. It's where you identify all the cool

---

* The 'Three C's Program' will be adapted and be available for purchase as an online course via my website www.zillacarina.com in the near future

bits that make you, *you* and all the things that light you up, including your dreams and goals. It clarifies all you need to enable you to move forward into the next phase of your life.

## COURAGE:

This is where you begin to release attachments you no longer need to allow you to feel strong enough to break down barriers standing in your way. We create courage through several strategies to disassemble, review and create new pathways to maintain your integrity and be true to your authentic self. We identify your passion(s) and how you can make a difference not only in your own life, but those near and dear to you as well.

## CONTINUITY:

This is where we create consistency and continuity by introducing new ways to ensure your stay on track. Here is where the key to long term success and transformation gets implemented. We build the foundations and establish deep roots and footings for stability in the first two phases of the program to create your success.

Thank you for coming along on this journey. In case you are wondering, I am well on my path to peace and freedom once again, and I will proudly wear the scars I've collected and carry them with me to the end of my days. They have given me knowledge and resilience and made me the person I am today, and this person is evolving and growing every day. This is only part of my story. I choose to continue to write fresh new pages and chapters every day, and I do it my way. For the first time in a very long time, I am super excited! I'm not exactly sure what the future looks like, but I'm ready to find out.

I feel fortunate and grateful every day I wake up another day older, and most days a teeny bit wiser. I look forward to having no regrets when the end of my days arrives. Here's a cheers to you for making it to this point, and to living your life consciously and to the full. Now, it's over to you to make the decisions you need to make and move towards living your best possible life.

Are you ready?

Q: What are three decisions you can make today to change your life and start creating your own future? How will you make sure you are accountable going forward? (eg, tell your commitment to a trusted friend, family member or someone independent who you can regularly check in with to hold yourself accountable to your new life).

Date: _____

_____

_____

_____

_____

# So, What Next?

We are all born with love in our hearts and need love to nurture our bodies and souls to grow. Unfortunately, so many have forgotten this. For a very long time, we have been dominated by dictators, leaders, politicians, and ego maniacs wanting world domination whether they be religious or driven by money and greed. These people use violence and destruction to get what they think they deserve; they believe they are better than others and use it as an excuse to destroy others. Unfortunately, innocent people and children who can't defend themselves are usually the first in the firing line. People who just want to live freely and enjoy life do not deserve this. How can we continue to allow this to happen? Today, we know better, we know the truth, we know we can do better. How much longer are we going to sit quietly and watch it happen?

We are all connected as beings on this planet. There is no point, or space for violence or hatred. No civilian in the world wants it. Every client I ask what they want for the world, they all say similar things—peace, love, clean planet, clean air and water. So why aren't governments listening? Are they so stuck in their outdated ways of thinking? Perhaps we could have a world referendum asking that same question? I believe there would be an overwhelming vote for peace and love across the planet.

My first and foremost recommendation is to start with ourselves. In order to work towards my personal mission—to raise the emotional frequency of humans on a global scale—we have to learn how to make peace from within first and create the ripple effect to those near and dear to us, then to friends and people we meet and by continuing to do this, it will traverse the planet. There are many healers and leaders already making great changes in the work they are doing, and those of us who are inspired to create a planet for generations to come will enable global change. Even if you have a positive effect on only a few people, they in turn will do the same and the ripple will begin to

## So, What Next?

accumulate and spread. I can already feel the positive feelings inside just thinking about helping even a few people to feel the same.

Please enjoy the first step to your journey of feeling positive and in tune with you by downloading the gift of my morning and evening mediations:

Your Morning Meditation

Your Evening Meditation

End Note:
Remember, no matter what/how we have been labelled in the past does not define our future. We have the power to choose how we show up in the world, and how we respond to any external environment and situation. Good or bad.

# About the Author

Zilla's journey is as diverse as it is captivating. Born in Sweden and transplanted to Australia at a young age, she embodies a unique blend of cultural influences and life experiences.

Zilla is a certified meditation teacher, results coach, advanced hypnosis practiotioner, speaker and author. Her expertise spans several decades and includes teaching/coaching individuals to inspiring audiences on stage, her passion for empowering others knows no bounds.

Having lived in multiple countries and travelled extensively, Zilla brings a global perspective to her work. Her experiences navigating different cultures and lifestyles have enriched her understanding of human resilience and potential.

Married three times and a mother to two incredible souls, Zilla knows a thing or two about navigating the highs and lows of relationships. Her own journey through what she affectionately refers to as going through "relationship hell and back, and then back to hell again" infuses her writing with raw authenticity and a deep understanding of behaviour patterns.

Armed with a degree in Environmental Science, Certificates in a variety of modalities, and certification as a Vedic Meditation Teacher, Zilla brings a unique perspective to everything she undertakes. Her experiences have shaped her into a compassionate and insightful guide for those seeking to overcome their own obstacles and create a life that is full and enriched.

Beyond her professional endeavours, Zilla finds her greatest joy in the simple pleasures of life. Whether she's spending quality time with her children or immersing herself in the energy of the ocean and the

## About the Author

serenity of the beach, she finds solace and inspiration in nature's embrace. An avid lover of mother nature, meditation, music, hiking, the beach, and skiing, Zilla is always seeking new adventures and experiences to enrich her journey and expand her own growth.

# Your Next Best Guest
## Zilla Carina ✨
### Author | Coach | Speaker

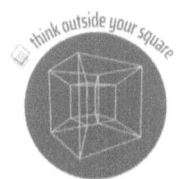

Meet Zilla, author, certified Coach, and Vedic Meditation Teacher with over three decades of corporate and coaching experience. She holds a Bachelor's Degree in Environmental Science and has mentored and trained over 1,000 individuals across various disciplines. Drawing from her own triumphs over personal challenges, Zilla believes in mastering our thoughts to shape our own life stories.

In her book, "The Scars We Carry," she explores resilience and using adversity as a catalyst for growth. Specialising in mindset, rapid results coaching, and meditation Zilla empowers people to proactively create lives they love. Her dynamic presence and powerful message inspire audiences to conquer challenges and foster positive change in their personal, family and lives and communities.

Zilla's dedication to conscious living and transformation underscores her mission to help others find clarity, courage and success. With a focus on empowering individuals to take charge of their destinies, she leaves a lasting impact by promoting mindfulness and personal growth in practical, actionable ways.

Zilla's dynamic presence and powerful message will leave your audience ready to conquer their own challenges.

FB/Insta: Zilla Carina
Email: hello@zillacarina.com
Website: zillacarina.com

### Zilla's Most Requested Topics:

**1: The Scars We Carry Book**
- Break free from denial and unlock your true self
- Use your scars as stepping stones to a brighter future
- Find your superpower and reclaim your life with joy, love, and peace

**2: Empower Yourself through Vedic Meditation**
- Create a mindset of healing, calm, and growth
- Utilize Vedic Meditation to foster personal transformation
- Develop inner peace and clarity to raise your frequency and realise your dreams

**3: From Fear to Freedom**
- Transform a life of fear into a life of freedom
- Overcome obstacles and embrace personal liberation
- Cultivate courage and resilience to pursue your aspirations

# Further Reading

(These are a few of my favourites. There are many more, find those that appeal and inspire you 💗)

Atomic Habits (James Clear, 2018)

Limitless, Expanded Version (Jim Kwik, 2023)

Breaking the Habit of Being Yourself – How to Lose Your Mind and Create a New One (Dr Joe Dispenza, 2012)

The Portal (Tom Cronin and Jacqui Fifer, 2019)

The Power of Now (Eckhart Tolle, 2004)

A New Earth (Eckhart Tolle 2005)

Think Like A Monk (Jay Shetty, 2020)

Ikigai (Hector Garcia and Francesc Miralles, 2016)

The Alchemist (Paolo Coelho, 1993)

The Prophet (Kahlil Gibran, 1923)

The Celestine Prophecy (James Redfield, 199…)

The Wisdom of Florence Scovel Shinn – 4 Complete Books ( Florence Scovel Shinn, 1989)

You Can Heal Your Life (Louise Hay, 1999)

The Tibetan Book of Living & Dying (Sogyal Rinpoche, 2002)

Zen and the Art of Motorcycle Maintenance (Robert M. Pirsig, 2006)

The Road Less Travelled (M. Scott Peck, 1978)

It's Not You – How to identify and Heal from NARCISSISTIC People (Dr Ramani Durvasula, 2024)

Blink (Malcolm Gladwell, 2005)

# Notes

# The Scars We Carry

# Notes

# The Scars We Carry

# Notes

www.ingramcontent.com/pod-product-compliance
Lightning Source LLC
Chambersburg PA
CBHW030037100526
44590CB00011B/245